CHRONICLERS OF
INDIAN LIFE

✛

TIME® LIFE BOOKS

Other Publications
VOICES OF THE CIVIL WAR
THE TIME-LIFE COMPLETE GARDENER
THE NEW HOME REPAIR AND IMPROVEMENT
JOURNEY THROUGH THE MIND AND BODY
WEIGHT WATCHERS® SMART CHOICE RECIPE COLLECTION
TRUE CRIME
THE ART OF WOODWORKING
LOST CIVILIZATIONS
ECHOES OF GLORY
THE NEW FACE OF WAR
HOW THINGS WORK
WINGS OF WAR
CREATIVE EVERYDAY COOKING
COLLECTOR'S LIBRARY OF THE UNKNOWN
CLASSICS OF WORLD WAR II
TIME-LIFE LIBRARY OF CURIOUS AND UNUSUAL FACTS
AMERICAN COUNTRY
VOYAGE THROUGH THE UNIVERSE
THE THIRD REICH
MYSTERIES OF THE UNKNOWN
TIME FRAME
FIX IT YOURSELF
FITNESS, HEALTH & NUTRITION
SUCCESSFUL PARENTING
HEALTHY HOME COOKING
UNDERSTANDING COMPUTERS
LIBRARY OF NATIONS
THE ENCHANTED WORLD
THE KODAK LIBRARY OF CREATIVE PHOTOGRAPHY
GREAT MEALS IN MINUTES
THE CIVIL WAR
PLANET EARTH
COLLECTOR'S LIBRARY OF THE CIVIL WAR
THE EPIC OF FLIGHT
THE GOOD COOK
WORLD WAR II
THE OLD WEST

*For information on and a full description of any of the Time-Life Books
series listed above, please call 1-800-621-7026 or write:*
Reader Information
Time-Life Customer Service
P.O. Box C-32068
Richmond, Virginia 23261-2068

This volume is one of a series that chronicles the history and culture of the Native Americans. Other books in the series include:

The Cover: Sam Kills Two, a Lakota medicine man, adds the symbol for the year 1926 to a winter count that chronicled 131 years of tribal history through pictographs denoting a memorable event for each year. Such visual records supplemented the histories related by Indians and by people of other cultures who lived among them and told of their traditions.

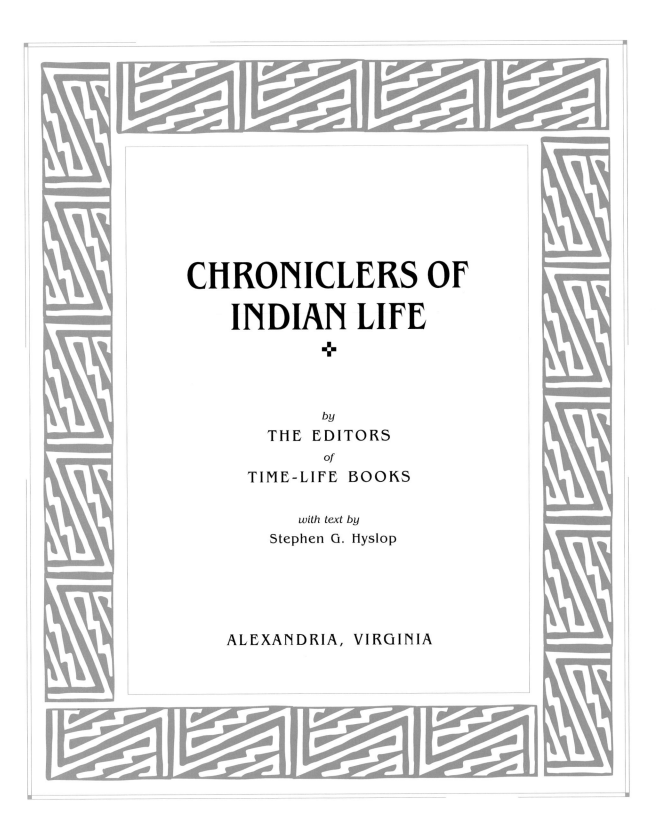

CHRONICLERS OF INDIAN LIFE

✛

by

THE EDITORS

of

TIME-LIFE BOOKS

with text by

Stephen G. Hyslop

ALEXANDRIA, VIRGINIA

Time-Life Books is a division of Time Life Inc.

PRESIDENT and CEO: John M. Fahey Jr.

TIME-LIFE BOOKS

MANAGING EDITOR: Roberta Conlan

Director of Design: Michael Hentges
Editorial Production Manager: Ellen Robling
Director of Operations: Eileen Bradley
Director of Photography and Research: John Conrad Weiser
Senior Editors: Russell B. Adams Jr., Janet Cave, Lee Hassig, Robert Somerville, Henry Woodhead
Library: Louise D. Forstall

PRESIDENT: John D. Hall

Vice President, Director of New Product Development: Neil Kagan
Associate Director, New Product Development: Elizabeth D. Ward
Marketing Director: Pamela R. Farrell
Vice President, Book Production: Marjann Caldwell
Production Manager: Marlene Zack
Quality Assurance Manager: Miriam P. Newton

THE AMERICAN INDIANS
SERIES EDITOR: Henry Woodhead
Administrative Editor: Loretta Y. Britten

Editorial Staff for *Chroniclers of Indian Life*
Senior Art Director: Dale Pollekoff
Picture Editor: Marion Ferguson Briggs
Text Editors: Stephen G. Hyslop (principal), John Newton
Associate Editors/Research-Writing: Jennifer Veech (principal), Robert H. Wooldridge Jr., Trudy W. Pearson
Senior Copyeditor: Ann Lee Bruen
Technical Art Assistant: Sue Pratt
Picture Coordinator: Daryl Beard
Editorial Assistant: Christine Higgins

Special Contributors: Marilyn Murphy Terrell (writing); Elizabeth Schleichert, Anne Whittle (research-writing); Douglas P. Baird, Barbara Fleming (research); Barbara L. Klein (index).

Correspondents: Christine Hinze (London), Christina Lieberman (New York), Maria Vincenza Aloisi (Paris). Valuable assistance was also provided by: Trini Bandrés (Madrid), Elizabeth Brown (New York), Barbara Gevene Hertz (Copenhagen), Angelika Lemmer (Bonn), Traudl Lessing (Vienna), Constance Richards (Moscow), Carolyn Sackett (Seattle).

Consultant
Frederick E. Hoxie is vice president for research and education at the Newberry Library in Chicago, and former director of its D'Arcy McNickle Center for the History of the American Indian. Dr. Hoxie is the author of *A Final Promise: The Campaign to Assimilate the Indians 1880-1920* (1984) and *Parading through History: The Making of the Crow Nation in America, 1805-1935* (1995), and editor of *Indians in American History* (1988) and *Discovering America* (1994). He has served as a history consultant to the Cheyenne River Sioux tribe, the Little Big Horn College Archives, and the Select Committee on Indian Affairs of the U.S. Senate. He is a founding trustee of the Smithsonian Institution's National Museum of the American Indian in Washington, D.C.

Special Consultant
W. Jackson Rushing is associate professor of art history at the University of Missouri-Saint Louis. He is the author of *Native American Art and the New York Avant-Garde* and coauthor of *Modern by Tradition: American Indian Painting in the Studio Style.* His essays on 20th-century art have been published in numerous journals and exhibition catalogs.

Library of Congress Cataloging in Publication Data
Chroniclers of indian life / by the editors of Time-Life Books.
    p. cm. — (The American Indians; 23)
    Includes bibliographical references and index.
    ISBN 0-8094-9733-6
    1. Indians of North America—History. 2. Indians of North America—Social life and customs. I. Time-Life Books. II. Series.
E77.C545 1996   95-45627
305.897'-dc20   CIP

CONTENTS

1
FROM CAPTIVITY TO KINSHIP

2
PORTRAYING THE PEOPLE

3
VOICES FROM THE HOMELANDS

ESSAYS

A PHOTOGRAPHER'S QUEST

On a summer day in 1900, photographer Edward S. Curtis, accompanied by naturalist George Bird Grinnell, rode to a rocky hilltop overlooking the plains of western Montana and gazed down on a breathtaking scene. There below them, hundreds of Blackfeet were camped with members of other tribes for their annual Sun Dance. "Neither house nor fence marred the landscape," Curtis wrote, and the rolling prairie was "carpeted with tipis." To the 32-year-old photographer, who up to that time had made a living portraying fashionable residents of Seattle, "the sight of that great encampment of prairie Indians was unforgettable." The scene helped inspire Curtis to compile a "photographic history of the American Indian," as he put it, a task that consumed him for nearly 30 years.

Intent on documenting traditions that persisted among native peoples despite the many changes they were undergoing, Curtis crossed the West time and again. In all, he visited 80 tribes and took 40,000 photographs, more than 1,500 of which appeared in his epic 20-volume series, *The North American Indian.* Curtis often returned two or three times to the same tribe in search of fresh images, sending an assistant ahead to prepare people for his visit and seeking the help of tribal elders when he arrived. When not taking pictures, he made notes on Indian customs and beliefs for the text that accompanied his photographs. In his eagerness to penetrate tribal circles, Curtis sometimes met with resistance. By his own reckoning, he was shot at four times during his travels. But most Indians welcomed him and allowed him to record moments of great power and intimacy. Like all gifted chroniclers, he owed much to the people who revealed themselves through his work. Only with their blessing was he able to capture not just their "vigorous outward existence," as Theodore Roosevelt wrote in tribute to him, but glimpses of their inner world "such as few white men ever catch."

E dward Curtis took this self-portrait in Seattle in 1899, at the age of 31. By then, he had visited and portrayed Indians around Puget Sound, but it was not until he traveled to Montana in 1900 that he dedicated himself to amassing a full photographic record of the western tribes—a sample of which appears on these pages, accompanied by Curtis's own titles.

THE TULE GATHERER—COWICHAN

outdoor sport" of the state's early settlers, he added, "was the killing of the Indians." Yet among the Hupa of California, as among tribes of the Pacific Northwest, people who remembered such deeds nonetheless took Curtis in and shared with him the ceremonies that renewed their world.

DANCING TO RESTORE AN ECLIPSED MOON—QA'GYUHL (KWAKIUTL)

*T*n the Southwest, Curtis portrayed tribal groups who had faithfully preserved customs of great antiquity. In northern New Mexico, he visited the Zia Pueblo, where people were still performing the Buffalo Dance although the animal itself had all but disappeared. In "Navaho-land," he observed,

ZIA BUFFALO MASK

"blanket looms are in evidence everywhere," much as they were centuries earlier. The once defiant Apache had submitted to federal authority by the time he arrived, but he still saw in mounted Apaches evidence of their fearlessness and "long resistance to subjection."

THE BLANKET WEAVER—NAVAHO

THE STORM—APACHE

On the rugged Plateau, nestled between the Rockies and the Cascades, Curtis met with peoples who looked in part for their livelihood to the Pacific Ocean and the fish that surged up the rivers and streams each year to spawn. As illustrated here, however, tribes of the

KLAMATH WOMAN

HOLIDAY TRAPPINGS—CAYUSE

region also drew support and inspiration from lands to their east, having long made "annual incursions into the buffalo plains," as Curtis put it. Like their neighbors on the Plains, many Plateau groups he visited still camped in tipis and delighted in displaying their riding skills and regalia.

*P*lains Indians offered much for Curtis to portray. He documented the persistence of tradition in the sweat lodge rituals of the Piegan Blackfeet and the finery of a young Oto. But he also conveyed a deep sense of loss in his portrait of Chief Red Cloud of the Oglala Sioux, shown here in 1905 in his eighties. "His

BRINGING THE SWEAT LODGE WILLOWS - PIEGAN

thoughts are of the past," Curtis said of the former war leader, who had forced the federal government to come to terms with the Sioux in 1868 only to see the territory reserved for them whittled down and his people impoverished. "His wish is ever that he might have passed away ere he knew the beggary of today."

A LITTLE OTO

RED CLOUD—OGLALA

*D*rawn to Alaska, where people still subsisted much as their ancestors had, Curtis observed the Nunivak and other Eskimos, or Inuit, struggling to gain their livelihood from the sea. In the spring, with the "breaking-up of the great ice-fields," he noted, "they go forth in their

THE IVORY CARVER—NUNIVAK

HOOPER BAY YOUTH

skin craft in quest of the food so long needed, buffeted constantly by sweeping gales." Their resilience and good cheer in the face of such hardships deeply impressed Curtis, who wrote that he had never encountered "a happier or more thoroughly honest and self-reliant people."

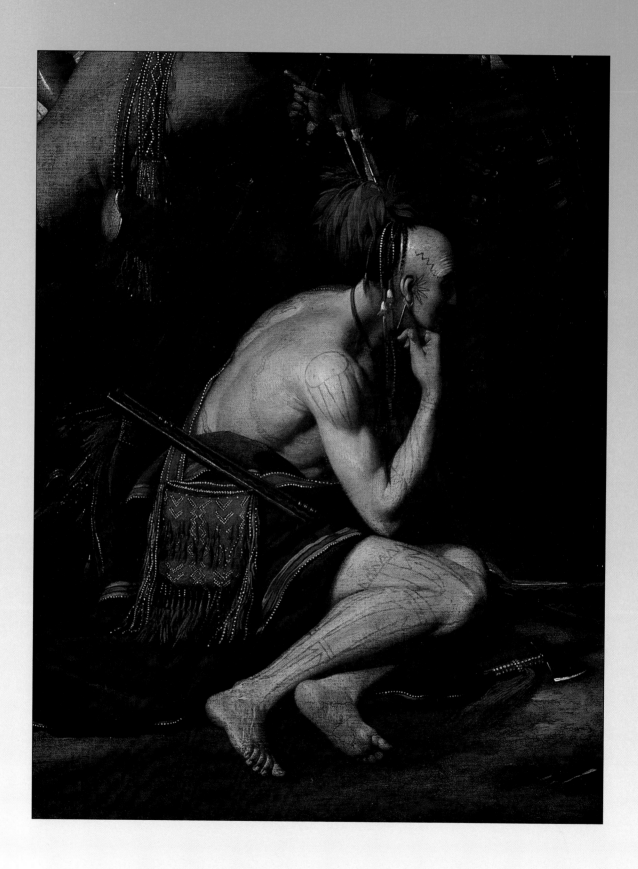

1

FROM CAPTIVITY TO KINSHIP

An Iroquois warrior crouches watchfully in the company of English soldiers in this detail from a painting by Benjamin West depicting action in 1759 during the French and Indian War. Part of a wider European struggle called the Seven Years' War, the conflict pitted the English and their allies against the French and Indians of many tribes, who seized and adopted a number of colonists, exposing them to a new way of life.

In May 1755, a young man from Pennsylvania named James Smith set out unwillingly on a revealing journey across a great cultural divide. Captured and adopted by Indians, he became part of their world in a way no mere visitor could. Smith fell prisoner at the age of 18, while serving with a crew of civilians who were clearing a road for English troops through the mountains of western Pennsylvania during the early stages of the French and Indian War, which saw many tribes of the eastern woodlands join with their French trading partners in opposing the land-hungry English. Smith and another settler were riding to hurry up provisions for the road crew when they were ambushed by three warriors, who opened fire with muskets from behind a screen of bushes, toppling Smith from his rearing horse and killing his companion.

Two of Smith's captors were Delawares, whose people had been swept by the tide of settlement from their ancestral homeland along the Delaware River. The third belonged to a group called the Caughnawaga, or Kahnawake, composed of Mohawks and other Iroquois who had settled in a Catholic mission village near the French at Montreal. The Caughnawaga was the first to lay hands on Smith, who thus became the property of that group, to dispose of as they saw fit.

Unlike many soldiers taken by Indians during the conflict, Smith escaped execution, perhaps because he had not been engaged in combat, or perhaps because his captors appreciated his youth and spirit and saw him as an ideal candidate for adoption. But he did not come through unscathed. The warriors led him to Fort Duquesne, a French stronghold at present-day Pittsburgh, where he was forced to run a gantlet of Indians armed with clubs. One of his captors advised him in English to hurry through as fast as he could to lessen the punishment. Smith did as he was told, but he was temporarily blinded by sand cast in his eyes and thrashed so hard that he passed out. Before fainting, Smith wrote afterward, he prayed that the Indians would "strike the fatal blow, for I thought they intended killing me, but apprehended they were too long about it." In fact, for captives like Smith who were considered worth sparing, such hazing

was the first stage of a lengthy initiation process that transformed the lowly prisoner into a respected member of the tribe.

After Smith recovered from the ordeal at Fort Duquesne, he was taken to an Indian village called Tullihas, along the west branch of the Muskingum River in Ohio. There, Caughnawagas who had left their community near Montreal when war broke out were living with uprooted Delawares. The day after he arrived at the village, Smith found himself at the center of a bewildering ritual. "A number of Indians collected about me," he wrote, "and one of them began to pull the hair out of my head. He had some ashes on a piece of bark, in which he frequently dipped his fingers in order to take the firmer hold, and so he went on, as if he had been plucking a turkey."

Smith was left with just three slender locks of hair dangling from the crown of his scalp, two of which were done up in a roach and the other braided and decorated with silver ornaments. "After this," he reported, "they bored my nose and ears, and fixed me off with earrings and nose jewels, then they ordered me to strip off my clothes and put on a breech-clout, which I did; they then painted my head, face and body in various colors."

Haunted by memories of captive soldiers he had seen put to death at Fort Duquesne, Smith feared that he was being prepared for his own exe-

James Smith (left), attacked while serving with a road crew on the frontier in Pennsylvania in 1755, is subdued by two Indian warriors while a third scalps Smith's slain companion. This engraving appeared in an early edition of Smith's account of the years he spent as an adopted captive of the Caughnawaga (known today as the Kahnawake), an Iroquois group allied with the French.

cution. In a sense, he was right, for the ceremony marked the end of his former existence and his rebirth as a Caughnawaga. As a crowd gathered around, an old chief held him by the hand and spoke to him solemnly, then entrusted him to three young women, who led him down to the river and gestured to Smith to immerse himself. He stubbornly refused, suspecting that the Indians meant to drown him and that the women were to be the executioners. "They all three laid violent hold of me, and I for some time opposed them with all my might, which occasioned loud laughter by the multitude that were on the bank of the river." Finally, one of the women managed to make her intentions clear to Smith in broken English—"no hurt you." At that, he yielded to the women, who were "as good as their word; for though they plunged me under water, and washed and rubbed me severely, yet I could not say they hurt me much."

Thus baptized, Smith emerged from the river and was conducted to the council house, where he donned new clothes, including a ruffled shirt, leggings, moccasins, and garters embroidered with beads and porcupine quills. He was seated on a bearskin rug and presented with a pipe, a tomahawk, and a hide pouch filled with tobacco and other gifts. His costume and equipment marked him as a figure of some distinction. As Smith soon learned from a Caughnawaga chief, who addressed him through an interpreter, he had been accepted into their ranks to take the place of an honored man who had recently died. "My son," the chief proclaimed, "you are now flesh of our flesh, and bone of our bone. By the ceremony which was performed this day, every drop of white blood was washed out of your veins; you are taken into the Caughnawaga nation, and initiated into a warlike tribe; you are adopted into a great family, and now received with great seriousness and solemnity in the room and place of a great man."

By entering the tribe in this fashion, Smith gained precious insights that eluded casual observers of Indian life. Too often, outsiders caught a fleeting glimpse of tribal customs

In an 18th-century engraving, prisoners run a gantlet of Iroquois waiting outside their village with clubs in hand. Smith endured a similar reception at Fort Duquesne, held by the French and their Indian allies. The demeanor of captives during such ordeals sometimes determined whether they would be executed or adopted.

A tribesman relaxes with a pipe outside his lodge while his wife tends to the children in this late-18th-century French depiction of an Iroquois encampment of the sort Caughnawagas maintained while away from their home settlement. An accompanying panel (below) shows details from the scene, including adornments for the head and ears, along with a powder horn, woven bag, cradleboard, musket, pipe tomahawk, and moccasins.

and pronounced them "savage" or "barbaric," either because they failed to understand what they witnessed or because they dealt with Indians strictly as enemies and saw only their hostile side. Smith himself was frightened and disoriented when he was first submerged in a strange culture. Only after many months among the Caughnawaga did he begin to fathom their wisdom and dedication. Like other chroniclers who entered tribal circles by chance, he first had to shed old misconceptions and misgivings before he could emerge as a discerning witness of the society.

Captives such as Smith, schooled in tribal values, were among the first to convey the richness and complexity of native cultures to the outside world. But not all chroniclers of Indian life were unwilling participants. Over the years, as cultural barriers came down, tribes were visited by dedicated ethnographers. Those keen observers lived as guests among Indians and documented their traditions with the help of astute tribal informants, who did much to shape the written record. And in recent times, many Native Americans have set down in writing their own instructive accounts, drawing on longstanding tribal traditions of storytelling and recordkeeping to inspire their people and enlighten outsiders.

In the strife-torn world that James Smith grew up in, however, few chroniclers bridged the gap of ignorance and hostility separating whites from Indians. Smith crossed that cultural divide and offered insightful

This halter made by Caughnawagas to restrain prisoners features an alluring design on the outside—and sharp porcupine quills on the inside, ensuring the compliance of captives. The device was recovered from a Massachusetts battlefield in the mid-1700s.

testimony because he was adopted—a ritual that was practiced in various forms by many native groups. Adoption gave Smith a secure position among the Caughnawaga. But it did not in itself prepare him to take the place of a great man. To be worthy of that honor, he first had to undergo a lengthy apprenticeship under the supervision of his elders. He was not asked to join in war parties, but he was expected to prove himself as a man by excelling as a hunter.

That summer, he went out with a hunting party led by a chief called Asallecoa, or Mohawk Solomon. In those days, small numbers of buffalo still roamed the woods and clearings below Lake Erie, and the chief offered him an unforgettable lesson in tracking that animal. Spotting some hoofprints, Smith ventured that they were surely those of a buffalo. "Hush, you know nothing," Mohawk Solomon scolded him in English, "may be buffalo tracks, may be Catawba." The chief explained that Catawbas from the Carolinas—longtime foes of the Iroquois—had once tied buffalo hoofs to their feet and made tracks in the soil to lure Caughnawagas into a deadly ambush. Not until Solomon came upon a fresh pile of buffalo dung did he let down his guard with a smile. "Catawba cannot make so," he assured Smith.

By this time, the Caughnawagas had armed Smith with a gun, but he soon gave them reason to doubt that he was mature enough to be trusted with one. Hunting on his own one day, he became disoriented and failed to find his way back to camp before the sun set. Stranded in the dark, he panicked and began shouting for help and firing his gun wildly into the air. When Caughnawagas finally tracked him down, they could tell by his circuitous path that he had not been trying to escape, but they confiscated the gun and confined him to a bow and arrow until he was wiser in the ways of the woods.

That fall, Smith was entrusted to another guardian, Tontileaugo, whom he referred to as his "adopted brother." Tontileaugo treated Smith as a member of the family, albeit one who still required quite a bit of looking after. Since Tontileaugo knew no English, Smith had to learn the Caughnawaga dialect in order to communicate. From that time forward, his companions referred to him by his Indian name, Scoouwa.

This model of a bark canoe complete with a miniature paddler, made by a Huron artist in the 19th century, resembles actual vessels crafted in earlier times. Such lightweight and sturdy craft gave Indians of the woodlands tremendous range in traveling the watersheds of the Northeast.

Smith joined Tontileaugo's hunting party of two dozen or so men, women, and children, who traveled together in a birch-bark canoe about 35 feet long. Come evening, Smith related, he and his companions dragged the vessel ashore, "turned the bottom up, and converted it to a dwelling house." He found that "with our baggage and ourselves in this house we were very much crowded, yet our little house turned off the rain very well." As winter approached, Tontileaugo's party buried their canoe to preserve it through the stormy months ahead and built a scaffold on which to drape the furs they had taken during the fall. Once again, Smith misinterpreted their preparations as hostile and feared the Indians meant to hang him from this makeshift "gallows," as he called it.

During the journey, Smith had been keeping a diary, which he carried with some books in a hide pouch. Recently, the books had disappeared, and Smith concluded that he had angered his hosts by reading the mysterious volumes "and that they were about putting me to death." In fact, the books aroused little more than curiosity among the Indians, who suspected that some of the puppies in camp had made off with Smith's pouch. Sure enough, one member of the party discovered the bundle nearby when they came back the following spring to retrieve their canoe. Smith was deeply gratified, and for the first time, he felt his heart warm to his Indian companions for graciously returning his books. "They knew I was grieved at the loss of them," he conceded, and "they rejoiced with me because they were found."

It was just one of many memorable lessons that Smith absorbed during his apprenticeship. Once during the winter, as he and others were carrying heavy loads of meat back to their camp in the Ohio woodlands, he put part of his burden down, promising to come back for it later. His companions laughed at him and gave the meat that he set aside to a woman who was already hauling as much as Smith. Like others of the tribe who sometimes found their lot hard to bear, Smith discovered that such public humiliation did more "to excite me to exert myself in carrying without complaining, than if they had whipped me for laziness."

A female doll of Indian design, outfitted for winter travel with snowshoes and a cradleboard secured to her toboggan, sports a silver gorget and a trade blanket—articles of European origin that were common among many eastern tribes by the 18th century.

Smith also learned to endure hunger patiently—and to feast heartily when he had the chance. After he and Tontileaugo killed a bear by smoking it out of the hollow of a tree, they cut up their prey on the spot and roasted the liver and other choice parts. "After I was fully satisfied I went to sleep," Smith recalled. But Tontileaugo roused him a short time later and urged him to make the most of this blessing, saying to him, "Come eat hearty, we have got meat plenty now."

If it was incorrect to pass up an opportunity for feasting, Smith discovered, it was positively rude to withhold any part of one's bounty from guests. During his second summer among the Caughnawaga, while Tontileaugo was away from camp, Smith was visited by a man of the Wyandot: western Hurons with whom Tontileaugo was allied by marriage. Smith gave the visitor some venison but failed to offer him the tasty mixture of bear oil and maple sugar that Caughnawagas carried to dip the meat in. The Wyandot thanked Smith politely for the meal, but Tontileaugo later scolded him for his stinginess, reminding him forcefully "that when strangers come to our camp, we ought always to give them the best that we have." Smith acknowledged his error, and Tontileaugo excused him on account of his youth but urged him thenceforth "to behave like a warrior, and do great things, and never be found in any such like actions." Smith was similarly scolded after helping some Indian women hoe a field—an activity that was out of keeping for any young man, let alone one who aspired to greatness.

In the fall of 1756, after he had been with the Caughnawaga more than a year, Smith was approached by "another adopted brother," as he put it, an older man named Tecaughretanego, who invited him on a hunt. By now, Smith realized that he was being treated as a free man and had the right to accept or decline this invitation. He replied tactfully that he was much "attached to Tontileaugo" but would consider the offer. Smith then had the courtesy to consult Tontileaugo, who assured him that Tecaughretanego was a "chief, and a better man than he was." With that gracious endorsement, Smith accepted the offer and went off with the elder brother, who shared with him not only his knowledge of the natural world but also the wisdom he had acquired as a medicine man. The Caughnawaga as a group had welcomed French priests and adopted Christianity. But the chief explained to Smith that he had never seen eye to eye with the priests and remained convinced that the "Indians' old religion was better than this new way of worshiping God."

Smith received constant encouragement and instruction from his new guardian. That winter, Smith again became lost in the woods, this time in a raging snowstorm. Keeping his wits about him, he imitated a bear and holed up in the hollow of a tree until the storm subsided. When he returned to camp and told his tale of survival, Tecaughretanego praised him for living up to the memory of the man he had been adopted to replace: "We are glad to see you on your own account, and we are glad to see the prospect of your filling the place of a great man."

An even sterner test awaited Smith the following winter, when the snow crusted over and he was unable to pursue game with any stealth. Camped with the ailing Tecaughretanego and a young kinsman who was only 10 years old, Smith saw no way of providing for them. He grew so despondent that the chief was moved to remind him that the "great being

An Indian on horseback draws his bow to finish off a wounded buffalo in this detail from a hide painting done in colonial times by a tribal artist in the Great Lakes area. Bison were still common, if not plentiful, in the region as recently as the late 1700s.

Tecaughretanego, a Caughnawaga chief and medicine man who embraced the captive James Smith as his adopted brother, appears at top in an engraving from Smith's account wearing a bear-claw necklace, a token of distinction among many woodlands tribes. Among the mysteries to which the chief introduced Smith was the ritual use of tobacco, stored in hide pouches like the one above, crafted by a Caughnawaga in the 1700s.

above feeds his people and gives them their meat in due season." It was sometimes necessary to suffer want, the chief added, in order to "know the worth of the favors that we receive." Despite that good counsel, Smith grew increasingly anxious. Finally, when he was off hunting alone one day, he decided to abandon his starving companions and hazard the long and uncertain journey back to Pennsylvania on his own. As he left the camp behind, however, he chanced upon a buffalo and brought it down with his gun. After roasting some of the meat and slaking his own hunger, he recalled the chief's words. Smith suddenly felt ashamed for deserting those who depended on him. Reflecting on his own "hardheartedness and ingratitude," he returned with his catch and cooked up a meal for Tecaughretanego and the boy. In the days ahead, hunting improved and the starving time receded into memory.

When spring arrived, the chief built a sweat lodge and conducted a ceremony to thank the Great Spirit for the recent blessings and to pray for bounty in the future. As he chanted, he burned the last of his tobacco in thanksgiving instead of smoking it. Smith, who knew how the old man enjoyed his tobacco, could not resist laughing when he saw it go up in smoke. The chief was deeply hurt, and Smith readily apologized, smoking some bark in a pipe with his elder brother as a gesture of reconciliation. But he did even more to atone years later, after he had returned to live among whites, when he paraphrased in print what the chief said to him. They were words that spoke eloquently to all those who persisted in making light of native people and their ceremonies.

"Brother, I have somewhat to say to you, and I hope you will not be offended when I tell you of your faults. You know that when you were reading your books in town, I would not let the boys or anyone disturb you. But now when I was praying, I saw you laughing. I do not think that you look upon praying as a foolish thing—I believe you pray yourself. But perhaps you may think my mode, or manner of praying foolish. If so, you ought in a friendly manner to instruct me, and not make sport of sacred things."

James Smith left the Caughnawaga with their consent in 1759, when he became one of a group of captives exchanged for French prisoners taken by the English during the war. It would be another 40 years before he transformed his journal entries into a book, and for much of that time, he pursued a military career that seemingly ran at odds with the sympathy he had developed for Indians while living among them. Returning to Pennsylvania, he formed a company of rangers in 1763 to battle tribes that supported Chief Pontiac of the Ottawa—an ally of the recently defeated French—who continued to wage war against the English. Smith dressed and painted his white volunteers as Indians and led them in Indian-style raids. Later, he used similar methods against tribes opposed to the American colonists during the Revolutionary War. When Smith got around to composing his story at the end of the century, he did so in part to persuade the public that Indians were disciplined and resourceful enemies and should be dealt with as such. "They are a sharp, active kind of people," he wrote, "and war is their principal study." Under the circumstances, he concluded, American troops would do well to adopt Indian tactics.

Although Smith was sincerely respectful of Indians as warriors, he shaded the truth when he claimed that fighting was "their principal study." He knew from experience that Indians had other endeavors that were no less important to them, including hunting, horticulture, and

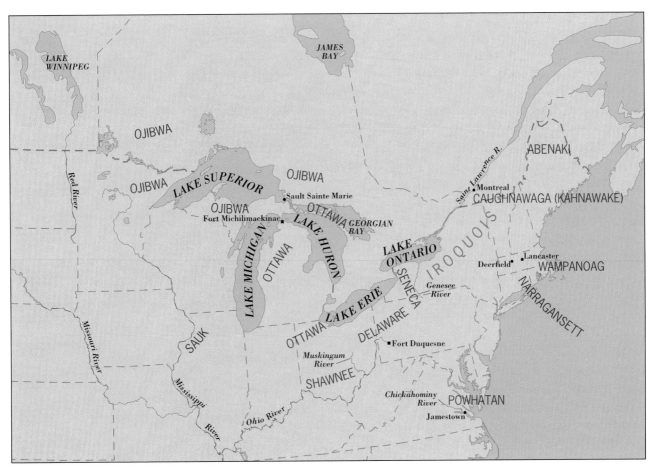

This map shows the locations of major land-marks and tribal groups described in the accounts of colonists who were captured and adopted by Indians during struggles for control of the northeastern woodlands. By the late colonial period, some groups such as the Delaware had already been forced westward from their ancestral homelands.

medicine of both the practical and spiritual kind. Like many who were captured and adopted by Indians over the years and told of the experience in writing, however, Smith was less concerned with offering a balanced portrait of Native American customs than with commanding the attention of readers and making a point. Some former captives wrote of their ordeals in order to praise God and to demonstrate that faith had seen them through. Others told of their adventures simply to pique the curiosity of the public and gain some profit or notoriety. Whatever their motives, all those who were drawn into tribal circles and wrote honestly of what they encountered helped sweep away tired myths about Indians and lay the groundwork for a genuine understanding of their way of life. These chroniclers told of truths impressed on them by tribal groups who as yet had been afforded little chance to speak directly to whites but who shaped the messages of those they adopted.

In one way or another, Indians have been captivating whites and molding their observations since explorers first reached the New World and began making entries in logs and journals. For it was only through interaction with tribal peoples that the early visitors to America made sense of what they saw. Some pioneering soldiers, traders, and missionaries absorbed valuable lessons about native warfare, religion, and daily life. But few outsiders got closer to Indians in the early days and learned more about their culture than those who met with misfortune and were taken in by them.

Such was the experience of Alvar Núñez Cabeza de Vaca, a member of an early Spanish expedition that came to grief along the Gulf Coast in 1528. That November, Cabeza de Vaca and several other shipwrecked Spaniards cast up on an island near what is now the Texas-Louisiana border, where they would almost certainly have died of hunger and exposure had they not been apprehended by Indians. Like other Europeans who later found themselves at the mercy of tribespeople, Cabeza de Vaca at first feared for his life and thought his hosts were feeding and sheltering him simply to prepare him for the "sacrificial knife." Instead, he suffered a more prosaic fate—he became part of the tribe and had to live as they did, eking out a meager living by fishing and foraging for roots. He considered this a form of slavery, but his life was not without rewards. The Indians assumed that these otherworldly Spaniards possessed special power, or medicine, and paid them for performing healing rites. Cabeza de Vaca and company were thus among the first Europeans to enter into the rich spiritual life of Native Americans. They also bore witness to the deep devotion of Indian parents for their children. "These people love their offspring more than any in the world and treat them very mildly," he wrote. "If a son dies, the whole village joins the parents and kindred in weeping."

After living for several years among Indians on the Gulf Coast, Cabeza de Vaca and several other Spaniards—including one man of North African an-

This kachina doll represents a Pueblo warrior spirit known as Chakwaina. The dark-featured Chakwaina may reflect tribal memories of Estevánico, a Moor who accompanied Alvar Núñez Cabeza de Vaca on his trek across the Southwest and later perished in a clash with Zunis in 1539.

cestry, a Moor named Estevánico, or Esteban—slipped away in 1534 and trekked west across Texas in the hope of reaching their compatriots in New Spain, as Mexico was then known. By this time, their reputation as healers had spread, and they attracted hundreds of Indian followers, who referred to them as Children of the Sun, a high compliment in a region where the sun was seen as the supreme source of earthly and spiritual power. Upon reaching an Indian village, the devoted throng told the inhabitants that the Spaniards had the "power to save or destroy" and demanded that the villagers offer goods as tribute to the medicine men and their entourage. Cabeza de Vaca called these followers "plunderers," but they sincerely believed in the medicine of the Spaniards. Before meals, he wrote, "every Indian brought his portion to us to be breathed on and blessed before he would dare touch it." In later centuries, ethnographers would rediscover the truth that Cabeza de Vaca and his companions had stumbled on during their remarkable journey—that outsiders who entered tribal society, whether as captives or guests, could alter the culture in surprising and unsettling ways even as they documented it.

Cabeza de Vaca and his companions finally found their way to Mexico City in 1536, and he returned the following year to Spain, where he dedicated the story of his New World adventure to Emperor Charles V. Today his chronicle is prized as the first intimate account of Indian lifeways north of Mexico, but at the time, Europeans were more intent on exploiting native peoples than understanding them. Contemporaries seized on vague rumors related by Cabeza de Vaca and his companions of wealthy Indians living in golden cities somewhere north of New Spain. Those rumors led to mercenary Spanish expeditions into Pueblo country, one of which cost the life of Estevánico, who was attacked and killed by Zunis in 1539. More than three centuries later, ethnographer Frank Hamilton Cushing visited Zunis and found that they were still telling stories of the "black Mexican" who came from the south and perished.

Other early accounts by Europeans of their capture or confinement engendered similar misconceptions even as they revealed how Indians tried to reckon with outsiders and incorporate them. Captain John Smith of Virginia's pioneering Jamestown Colony, for example, offered a memorable if misleading account of his imprisonment by followers of the paramount chief Powhatan during the winter of 1607-1608. After being trapped in a swamp by Powhatan warriors while exploring the lower Chickahominy River, Smith was held in a longhouse and guarded by "30 or 40 tall fellows," who plied him with more bread and venison "than

The Countrey wee now call Virginia beginneth at Cape Henry distant from Roanoack 60 miles, where was S.ʳ Walter Raleighs plantation. and because the people differ very little from them of Powhattan in any thing, I have inserted those figures in this place because of the conveniency.

King Powhatan comands C. Smith to be slayn, his daughter Pokahontas beggs his life his thankfullnes and how he Subiected 39 of their kings reade y histo

Pocahontas, in apparent defiance of her father, Chief Powhatan (background, right), throws herself on the prostrate Captain John Smith to save him from harm in an illustration from Smith's chronicle of his days in captivity among Powhatan's people in the winter of 1607-1608. Smith's survival was probably decreed by Powhatan, who wanted to impress his authority on the English leader and adopt him as a subordinate chief.

would have served 20 men." Smith thought that they were fattening him up to feast on, and he left most of the food to the guards, who consumed the uneaten portion each morning before delivering more. Later, Smith was taken to another lodge and confronted by a priest he described as a "great grim fellow, all painted over with coal, mingled with oil." The priest wore an imposing headdress of snakeskins, weasel hides, and feathers and conducted a divination ceremony with the help of six attendants to see if the prisoner meant them well or ill. Finally, Smith was led before the paramount himself and threatened by men with clubs before Powhatan's young daughter Pocahontas purportedly rescued him.

By portraying Pocahontas as his savior, John Smith not only distorted the strong message Powhatan and his followers were sending him but also spawned an enduring legend. As a paramount chief with control over dozens of tribes and tens of thousands of people, Powhatan was at that time one of the most powerful Indian leaders in North America. If his daughter, who was still a child, acted kindly toward Smith and his fellow colonists, she was surely doing so at the behest of her father, who alternated threats with inducements in the hope of persuading the intruders to defer to him as their overlord.

Instead of heeding Powhatan's lesson and accepting his authority, however, Smith defied him in years to come and portrayed him in writing as a vacillating figure, prey to the whims of his daughter, who supposedly sided with the colonists out of sheer admiration for their superior qualities. In fact, it was only after Pocahontas was captured and indoctrinated by the English as a young woman that she truly embraced their ways. Nonetheless, Anglo-Americans followed Smith's lead and touted her as the prototype of the "good Indian," who freely abandoned her tribal values for those of English society. Presumably, many others would do the same, if offered the chance.

Experience taught otherwise. Along the East coast, Europeans faced strong opposition whenever their expanding settlements threatened tribal traditions or subsistence patterns. One of the boldest uprisings occurred in southern New England in 1675 when the Wampanoag chief Metacomet, referred to by colonists as King Philip, rallied traditionalists of his and other tribes against the English. In that conflict and in later clashes between whites and Indians over the next century, more than 1,500 colonists were taken prisoner by warriors in New England alone. Some war parties seized hostages for the same reason that whites often held Indians—to sell or ransom them at the best possible terms. But in many other cases, Indians captured whites in order to adopt them and replenish the tribe. That the taking of prisoners could be motivated by a constructive impulse was hard for some colonists to fathom, because they regarded Indians in simplistic terms, as either childishly innocent or irredeemably cruel. Captives who lived among Indians for any length of time, however, and were later ransomed or set free told of tribespeople who were as complex in their character and motivations as any group of Europeans.

One celebrated captivity story of the era was penned by New Englander Mary Rowlandson, who was taken prisoner by Wampanoags and allied Narragansetts during King Philip's War and held for nearly three months before being ransomed. Rowlandson's account became a bestseller and went through dozens of editions, in part because she portrayed her ordeal as punishment visited on her by God, a lesson that harmonized with the stern faith of many colonists. To reinforce her biblical theme, Rowlandson sometimes described the Indians as "heathens" and likened them to the pagan enemies sent by God to punish the Israelites for their sins. In other passages, Rowlandson characterized Metacomet's warriors as wild animals or devils. "It was a solemn sight to see," she wrote of her neighbors and relatives who died in the attack on her hometown of Lancaster, Massachusetts, in February 1675, "so many Christians lying in their blood, some here and some there, like a company of sheep torn by wolves." Afterward, she wrote, the men who took her captive sang and danced like "black creatures in the night, which made the place a lively resemblance of hell."

Despite such damning language, Rowlandson cited many instances during her captivity of kind treatment from Indians, who shared food with her when she was hungry and comforted her when she wept. Once, she was offered a warm, dry wigwam to sleep in while those watching over her spent the night out in the rain. Characteristically, she attributed this act of compassion to God rather than to the Indians. "Thus the Lord dealt mercifully with me many times," she wrote, "and I fared better than many of them." She also testified that she was never subject to sexual advances, either by the chief whose household she joined or by any other Indians. "I have been in the midst of those roaring lions, and savage bears," she wrote of her captors, "that feared neither God, nor man, nor the devil, by night and day, alone and in company; sleeping all sorts together, and yet not one of them ever offered the least abuse of unchastity to me, in word or action."

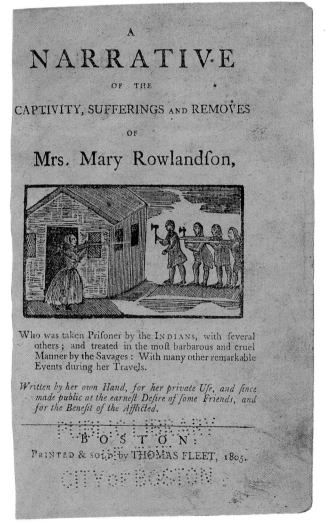

A woman defends her home against Indians on the frontispiece of Mary Rowlandson's narrative of her capture in 1675 by warriors of King Philip. Rowlandson said nothing in her account of firing on warriors and told of being treated with decorum by many Indians, branded here collectively as "savages."

A

NARRATIVE

OF THE

CAPTIVITY, SUFFERINGS AND REMOVES

OF

Mrs. Mary Rowlandſon,

Who was taken Priſoner by the INDIANS, with ſeveral others; and treated in the moſt barbarous and cruel Manner by the Savages: With many other remarkable Events during her Travels.

Written by her own Hand, for her private Uſe, and ſince made public at the earneſt Deſire of ſome Friends, and for the Benefit of the Afflicted.

B O S T O N:
PRINTED & SOLD by THOMAS FLEET, 1805.

CITY OF BOSTON

Beads of inlaid shell, or wampum, adorn this 17th-century war club, said to have belonged to the Wampanoag chief Metacomet, known to the English as King Philip. The war club was reportedly purchased by a colonist from an allied Indian who killed the chief in 1676, bringing to an end King Philip's War.

Again, Rowlandson saw this as God's work, thus overlooking the strictures that prevailed among the Indians and shielded her from abuse. Although it was not unheard of for warriors to rape captives, most tribes spurned the practice. Overall, white women taken prisoner by Indians stood far less risk of being raped than did Indian women seized by whites. Nevertheless, the mere threat of sexual abuse stirred up angry passions and transformed some later captivity stories by white women into fuel for murderous vendettas directed against Indians.

Rowlandson, it turned out, had more trouble with the women of the tribe than with the men, for the chief responsible for her, a relative of King Philip, had three wives, one of whom took a powerful dislike to her. "A severe and proud dame she was," Rowlandson wrote, "bestowing every day in dressing herself near as much time as any gentry of the land; powdering her hair, and painting her face, going with her necklaces, with jewels in her ears, and bracelets upon her hands." As a devout Puritan, Rowlandson disapproved of such vanity, but she was honest enough to admit that white gentry were much the same. Indeed, the region's tribes had a privileged class that was not unlike the English one. Rowlandson profited by its existence by fashioning articles of clothing for Philip and other tribal dignitaries, who paid for her services. Although she referred to her time among the Indians as a journey into the "howling wilderness," she never lost touch with society—albeit an Indian one, with its own virtues and foibles.

At times, Rowlandson was so touched by the memory of the favors Indians performed for her that she laid aside her sermonizing and wrote with plain gratitude. In particular, she recalled one couple who fed her repeatedly: "If I went to their wigwam at any time, they would always give me something, and yet they were strangers that I never saw before." An-

Birch bark and elm bark cover this recon- struction of an Algonquian lodge. Indian bands on the move during King Philip's War and other unsettled times quickly disassem- bled such bark-covered wigwams and car- ried the materials to their next campsite.

other Indian woman offered her a "piece of fresh pork, and a little salt with it, and lent me her frying pan to fry it; and I cannot but remember what a sweet, pleasant and delightful relish that bit had to me, to this day. So little do we prize common mercies, when we have them to the full."

Those captives who stayed longer among Indians than Rowlandson and were formally adopted into native families became all the more ap- preciative of their common mercies and sometimes refused to return to white society when they had the opportunity. Such was the case with young Eunice Williams, who was captured during an attack in 1704 on the English settlement of Deerfield, Massachusetts, by Abenaki and Caughnawaga warriors allied to the French. Some of her relatives died in the assault, and other family members were seized along with her— including her father, Reverend John Williams, who was ransomed after eight weeks in captivity and spent years trying to obtain her release from the Caughnawaga. By the time he finally succeeded in arranging for an English intermediary to visit Eunice at the Caughnawaga settlement near Montreal in 1713, she was 16 years old and married to a member of the tribe. She had forgotten English and had to be addressed through an interpreter. When the intermediary urged her to return to her white relatives in New England, she made it clear to him that she had found her family here among the Indians and would never abandon them.

That a captive would choose not to be redeemed shocked pious colonists like John Williams, who assumed that those who lived as the Indians did were beyond God's grace. Even groups like the Caughnawaga who accepted Catholicism were considered lost souls by Protestants, much as Indians who had been influenced by Protestant missionaries were regarded as heathens by Catholics. It remained to later witnesses to demonstrate that Indians could be profoundly religious without benefit of Christian clergy. James Smith learned as much from Tecaughretanego, the Caughnawaga chief and medicine man who rejected the observances of French priests in favor of the rituals of his ancestors. But even stronger testimony came from whites who were taken in by the devout Ojibwa of the Great Lakes region and felt the power of their convictions.

Caughnawaga and Abenaki Indians allied with the French burn the English settlement of Deerfield, Massachusetts, in this early engraving of an attack in 1704 that saw many of the town's inhabitants taken prisoner. One adopted captive, Eunice Williams, grew so close to the Caughnawagas that she refused to return home when offered the chance.

In the summer of 1762, an adventurous young Anglo-American trader by the name of Alexander Henry received an extraordinary offer from an Ojibwa named Wawatam. Henry had just begun dealing with Indians for furs at Fort Michilimackinac, situated at the juncture of Lakes Huron and Michigan and occupied by English troops at the close of the French and Indian War. Although the Ojibwa had sided with the opposing French, they seemed friendly enough to Henry—and none more so than Wawatam, a thoughtful man in his mid-forties, or nearly twice Henry's age.

One day, the trader wrote, Wawatam appeared at Henry's post with a generous gift of furs and food and commenced a long speech. "He informed me that some years before, he had observed a fast, devoting himself, according to the custom of his nation, to solitude and to the mortification of his body, in the hope to obtain from the Great Spirit protection through all his days; that on this occasion, he had dreamed of adopting an English-

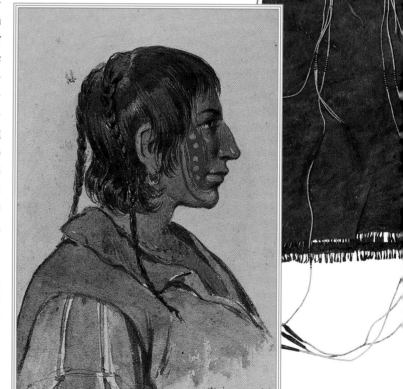

man as his son, brother, and friend; that from the moment in which he first beheld me, he had recognized me as the person whom the Great Spirit had been pleased to point out to him for a brother; that he hoped that I would not refuse his present; and that he should forever regard me as one of his family."

Wawatam's vision from the Great Spirit turned out to be a godsend for Henry. Fresh conflict was brewing in the region, and he would soon have desperate need of a guardian. The following June, local Ojibwas and some visiting Sauk Indians, who had quietly enlisted with them in Pontiac's campaign against the English, staged a surprise attack at Michilimackinac. As the troops there looked on placidly, men of the two tribes played a game of lacrosse to celebrate the king's birthday, then exchanged their sticks for concealed weapons in mid-contest and took the fort by storm. Although Henry hid out in the home of a French trader there, he was soon discovered and came close to being executed along with many of the captured British soldiers. He was spared only because Wawatam made an appeal to an Ojibwa kinsman, Chief Menehwehna, offering goods to buy off claims any other warriors might have on Henry's life. "I adopted him as my brother," Wawatam said of Henry. "From that moment, he became one of my family, so that no change of circumstances could break the cord which fastened us together."

Menehwehna honored Wawatam's appeal and placed Henry under his care. In the months ahead, the trader became an integral part of his guardian's family. Partly to protect

A portrait of an Ojibwa man reveals face paint and scalp lock stylings of the sort common when fur trader Alexander Henry was taken in by Ojibwas of the Great Lakes region in 1763 and adorned as a member of the tribe.

Beads, feathers, and shell breastplates ornament this early-19th-century shirt that was worn by a tribesman of the Great Lakes area.

Henry from warriors who had lost kin to the English and might seek his life in return, he was dressed as a member of the tribe. "My hair was cut off, and my head shaved, with the exception of a spot on the crown," he wrote. "My face was painted with three or four different colors; some parts of it red, and others black. A shirt was provided for me, painted with vermilion, mixed with grease. A large collar of wampum was put around my neck, and another suspended on my breast." Henry felt diminished without his full head of hair, "but the ladies of the family, and of the village in general, now condescended to call me handsome."

Dressing as an Ojibwa was only a superficial conversion. Henry's deeper indoctrination into the culture came that fall when he departed with Wawatam's family to their winter hunting ground in northern Michigan. There he found that what was for him a source of worldly profit—the taking of animals and their furs—was part of a deeper spiritual quest for Ojibwas, who regarded a successful hunt as a form of communion with transcendent powers. To track a beaver, he discovered, was to follow the spirit of a prodigiously gifted creature. Indeed, beavers had once been able to speak, Henry learned, but they had been deprived of that talent by Gitche Manitou, or the Great Spirit, "lest they should grow superior in understanding to mankind."

Respect for the spirit of the bear was even greater, as indicated by an elaborate ritual Wawatam's party conducted when they took their first bear of the season. Henry himself spotted the bear's den in the hollow of a tree and shot the animal when it emerged. Afterward, the Ojibwas stroked and kissed the bear's head, addressing the slain animal as "grandmother" and "begging a thousand pardons for taking away her life." They implored her "not to lay the fault upon them, since it was truly an Englishman that had put her to death." Later, the bear's head was placed on a scaffold and adorned with wampum and other treasure, and Wawatam and Henry blew tobacco smoke into its nostrils. Wawatam addressed the bear tenderly, deploring the "necessity under which men labored, thus to destroy their *friends.*" Once the creature's spirit had been properly honored, Henry noted, the Ojibwas felt no misgivings about feasting on it: "We all ate heartily of the bear's flesh, and even the head itself, after remaining three days on the scaffold, was put into the kettle."

When Wawatam's party brought their furs to a French trader the next spring, Henry discovered that all his labor during the winter had earned him only enough to purchase some new clothes, along with a fresh supply of ammunition and tobacco. Yet he had shared in other rewards that defied calculation—spiritual gains that sustained the Ojibwa through their difficult seasonal round. That summer, he parted company with Wawatam and traveled to Sault Sainte Marie aboard the canoe of Madame Cadotte, the Indian wife of a trader. He left in the hope of resuming his former life and did so with the full blessing of Wawatam, who prayed to Gitche Manitou "to take care of me, his brother, till we should next meet." As the canoe pulled away, Wawatam's voice faded into the distance, but Henry could still see him on the receding shore, offering up his prayers.

In the months ahead, Henry remained under the spell of Ojibwas and their beliefs. When his canoe reached Sault Sainte Marie, he found that Ojibwa chiefs and warriors there who had joined in Pontiac's War were being summoned to a great peace conference by the English, who were eager to restore trading ties with the hostile tribes. The Ojibwas feared reprisals if they attended the conference, however, and appealed for spiritual guidance. They made offerings of tobacco and had one of their priests conduct a shaking-tent ceremony, during which the holy man sought advice from the Great Turtle and other far-seeing spirits who rattled the tent mysteriously when they appeared.

Henry was initially skeptical of this "scene of imposture," as he called it. But after the spirits had assured the Indians through the priest that they would be treated well by the English, Henry could not resist inquiring as to whether he would safely return from Indian territory to the colonies and his Anglo-American countrymen: "I yielded to the solicitations of my own anxiety for the future; and having first, like the rest, made my offering of tobacco, I inquired, whether or not I should ever revisit my native country? The question being put by the priest, the tent shook as usual; after which I received this answer: 'That I should take courage and fear no danger, for that nothing would happen to hurt me; and that I should in the end reach my friends and country in safety.' " Henry was so pleased with this response that he offered the spirits extra tobacco.

The prophecy proved to be correct. After traveling with Ojibwas to Fort Niagara, he came under the protection of English authorities and later resumed his career as a trader among the Ojibwa. His year with Wawatam and family had introduced him to a world where people of great devotion adopted strangers and watched over them in much the same way that the spirits above looked after their relatives on earth. But his revealing experience was a mere dip into the culture compared with the prolonged immersion that awaited one John Tanner of Kentucky. Tanner was captured as a boy in 1789 and spent nearly 30 years among Ojibwas, growing so close to them in spirit that he even learned to dream as they did.

Tanner's life among the Indians began inauspiciously. Raised on an isolated homestead by a stern widower, Tanner was a rebellious child who often wished he could "go and live among the Indians," as he put it, assuming that he would then enjoy unbridled freedom. But after he was seized in a raid about the age of nine, he soon discovered that Indian boys were subject to their own exacting forms of discipline.

The warrior who captured Tanner and led him to a village in present-day Michigan did so to oblige his wife, who after the death of their youngest boy asked her husband to "bring back her son," which could only be done by adopting a replacement. At her first sight of young Tanner, the bereaved woman wept and embraced him as her own. The next day, he was led to the grave of the son who had died. There family and friends,

A memento of the fur trade, this finely quilled birch-bark box was crafted by an Ojibwa in 1834. The quillwork scenes depict beaver and other creatures of the lakes region as well as camp life and travel by canoe.

An Ojibwa band cooks a meal in camp on the American side of the rapids of Sault Sainte Marie in this painting by 19th-century Canadian artist Paul Kane. The abundance of fish at the rapids made it a gathering place for various tribes and for whites who were eager to trade with them.

standing on one side, waited with presents that Tanner himself distributed to guests on the other side of the grave in a ceremony that he described as strangely "cheerful, after the manner of the scalp dance." As he danced in a circle, the hosts gave him the gifts one by one, but as he "came around in dancing to the party on the opposite side of the grave, whatever they had given me was snatched from me: thus they continued a great part of the day, until the presents were exhausted."

This haunting ceremony proved to be prophetic of Tanner's future. As a replacement for the dead son, he was immediately acknowledged as part of the family and the community. But that honor carried with it many obligations, and Tanner, like all members of the tribe in these difficult times, would have to give as much as he received. The first demands he had to meet came from his new father and brothers, who asked him to prove he was worthy of acceptance by pulling his weight as a hunter. Unfortunately, Tanner antagonized his new guardian much as he had his natural father. On one dire occasion, he fell asleep in the woods when he was supposed to be building a blind to shoot deer from, so enraging his foster father that the man struck him in the head with a tomahawk and left him for dead, informing his mother that he was "good for nothing." His mother and sister retrieved him and nursed him back to health, but young Tanner never gained the respect of his male relatives. After two years, a prominent kinswoman of his father's named Netnokwa, who had also lost a son about Tanner's age, obtained custody of him over the protest of his mother by offering the family presents that included a "10-gallon keg of whiskey, blankets, tobacco, and other articles of great value."

Netnokwa was an Ottawa, but through long association and intermarriage, her people had become virtually a branch of the Ojibwa. Under her guardianship, Tanner found his lot much improved. Netnokwa "gave me plenty of food," he remarked, "put good clothes upon me, and told me to go and play with her own sons." Tanner described her as principal chief of the Ottawa. Whatever her actual position in the tribe, she had full command of her household, including her husband, who was a generation younger than Netnokwa and deferred to her in all matters. He too treated Tanner well and gave him his first gun. Once the boy became adept at hunting and trapping, he was "no longer required to do the work of the women about the lodge."

As Tanner grew older, however, the fortunes of his family declined. His stepfather died prematurely, as a result of a fight with another man while the two were drinking. The loss of an able-bodied man could mean deprivation for his kin, and Tanner's stepfather feared as much as he lay near death. "Now, my children, I have to leave you," he said. "I am sorry that I must leave you so poor." He did not ask his children to avenge him. As Tanner put it, "He was too good a man to wish to involve his family in the troubles which such a course would have brought upon them."

After his death, Netnokwa took her kin away from the Michilimackinac area, where they had lived for some time, to join relatives west of Lake Superior in the vicinity of Red River, below present-day Winnipeg. Many Ojibwas and Ottawas were moving west about this time, as whites intruded on their homeland and overhunting reduced the supply of game. Although the prospects for hunters and trappers were better in the Red River country, the winters there were even more severe, and Tanner and his kin faced tremendous hardship in the years ahead. The journey in itself was long and harrowing. The family wintered at the western end of Lake Superior and might have starved there had they not been taken in by a Muskogee—or Swamp Indian—who made room for the needy family in his lodge and hunted for them. "Such is still the custom of the Indians, remote from whites," Tanner observed years later. He added that near trading posts and settlements, however, some Indians had "learned to be like the whites and to give only to those who can pay."

The prevailing charity among Ojibwas helped persuade Tanner, who was now in his early teens and free to move about as he pleased, to remain with Netnokwa and kin: "I remembered the laborious and confined manner in which I must live if I returned among the whites; where, having no friends, and being destitute of money or property, I must, of necessity, be exposed to all the ills of extreme poverty. Among the Indians, I saw that those who were too young, or too weak to hunt for themselves, were sure to find someone to provide for them. I was also rising in the estimation of the Indians, and becoming as one of them." As a token of acceptance, his companions now referred to him by a tribal name meaning the "Falcon."

John Tanner, shown here in European-style clothing after he returned to live among whites about 1820, spent nearly three decades among Ojibwas and kindred Ottawas after being captured as a boy in Kentucky.

Furthermore, he was growing increasingly attached to his step-brother, Wamegonabiew, who was a few years older than Tanner, and to the redoubtable Netnokwa. "She could accomplish whatever she pleased, either with the traders or the Indians," Tanner remarked, "probably, in some measure, because she never attempted to do anything which was not right and just." She was also remarkably vigorous for her age. If a high wind came up when their canoe was still far from shore, she would first offer a "loud and earnest prayer to the Great Spirit," then apply herself "with surprising activity to the use of her paddle."

When the family finally reached the Red River country, they were warmly greeted by kindred Ojibwas and Ottawas. "These, our relations, have come to us from a distant country," one chief proclaimed. "We must not suffer them to be in want among us." At first, there was plenty for all, but the camp was a large one, and as winter closed in, game grew scarce. As she often did in times of want, Netnokwa prayed for guidance in her dreams. One morning, she informed her sons that the Great Spirit had visited her in the night and promised her that she would feast before the day was out on a bear, to be found "in a small round meadow, with something like a path leading from it."

Wamegonabiew disregarded the prophecy, but Tanner had yet to kill a bear and went in search of the place his mother told of. After some effort, he discovered a round clearing in the woods, with a brook running from it. There he literally stumbled on a den, falling through the snow up to his waist and uncovering the head of a hibernating bear, which he dispatched with a single blast from his gun. When Tanner told Netnokwa that her dream had come true, "she watched my face for a moment, and then caught me in her arms, hugging and kissing me with great earnestness." That night, all the band's hunters joined in the feast to honor the boy's first kill.

Despite this success, Tanner remained dubious of Netnokwa's gift. He suspected that such prophecies were based on her knowledge of the surrounding country—and in one case confirmed that a bear she dreamed of and directed hunters to was in fact one whose lair she had already located. In time, however, he himself began to meet with spirits in his dreams, and he became convinced of their prophetic power.

Tanner's first significant dream encounter came when he was about 20 years old and journeying to the Red River trading post on his own to obtain supplies for his kin. As he paddled his buffalo-skin canoe along a tributary of the Red River, he passed an inviting landing place that local

Indians had long avoided because one brother had killed another there and had later been executed and buried with the victim on the spot. Scornful of the tribal legend that said the spirits of the ill-fated brothers still haunted the place, Tanner kindled a fire there and lay down by the embers to sleep.

That night, in a fitful reverie, he "saw the two dead men come and sit down by my fire, opposite me. Their eyes were intently fixed upon me, but they neither smiled, nor said anything. I got up and sat opposite them by the fire, and in this situation I awoke. The night was dark and gusty, but I saw no men, or heard any other sounds than that of the wind in the trees.

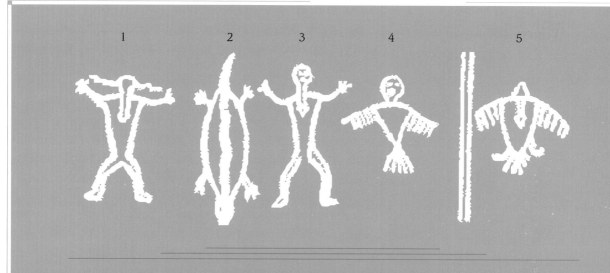

SACRED SONGS OF THE OJIBWA

John Tanner's education among the Ojibwa included instruction in the use and interpretation of pictographs, figures that were carved into pieces of wood or bark to record the text for sacred songs and prayers. Each picture denoted the subject of a verse, or phrase, whose actual words were committed to memory beforehand and then recalled in the proper order with the aid of the pictographs.

The pictographs above, reproduced in Tanner's account, represent the verses of a song chanted by Ojibwa medicine men in order to bring good fortune in the hunt. Figure one reminds the singer to begin the song by calling his friends and followers to listen to his entreaty. The second figure cues the singer to tell his audience of the Great Spirit who makes the river flow (symbolized by wavy lines on the back of a beaver). At figure three, the singer calls upon his listeners to look to him for leadership. Then he reveals himself as a shaman with the hunting power of a bird (fourth sign). Lines drawn between figures four and five indicate the moment for the singer to begin the accompanying dance steps. The last figure prompts him to sing that he will fly about in a vision like a bird to find game, thus demonstrating his sacred medicine for hunting.

Lines leading from the hearts of two moose and a bear represent the gift of life granted to John Tanner by a spirit who offered the animals to him in a dream during a time of great hunger. Upon awakening from his dream, Tanner drew the animals on bark to ensure that his vision would come true. Following the directions of his dream visitor, he tracked and killed two moose within hours.

It is likely I fell asleep again, for I soon saw the same two men standing below the bank of the river, their heads just rising to the level of the ground I had made my fire on, and looking at me as before. After a few minutes they rose one after the other, and sat down opposite me; but now they were laughing, and pushing at me with sticks, and using various methods of annoyance. I endeavored to speak to them, but my voice failed me. I tried to fly, but my feet refused to do their office."

One of the spirits then told him of a stray horse on a nearby hill and invited him to ride the animal to his destination and back, so "you can spend another night with us." Come morning, Tanner climbed that hill and found a lone horse belonging to the trader he was on his way to visit. He abandoned his canoe and rode the horse to the post. But he had learned to fear the spirits and never revisited the dreaded "place of the two dead."

Later in his life, when he and his Ojibwa kin were threatened with starvation, Tanner resorted to "medicine hunting" of the sort Netnokwa taught him. "Half the night I sung and prayed, and then lay down to sleep," he recalled of the first such vigil he conducted. "I saw in my dream a beautiful young man come down through the hole in the top of my lodge, and he stood directly before me. 'What,' said he, 'is this noise and crying that I hear? Do I not know when you are hungry and in distress? I look down upon you at all times, and it is not necessary you should call me with such loud cries.' " Then the young man gestured to the west and pointed out the tracks of two moose and a bear that were Tanner's for the taking. When he awoke, he smoked tobacco to honor this dream visitor and sketched the figures of the animals on a piece of birch bark. Then he took his gun and set off in the appointed direction. Well before noon, he reported, "I fell on the track of two moose, and killed them both, a male and a female, and extremely fat." This same dream visitor appeared to him repeatedly in years to come, to warn of danger or direct him to game.

Tanner's task as a hunter was made more difficult by the fact that he now had children to feed. In spite of his inclination as a young man to enjoy his freedom and put off marriage, he yielded in his early twenties to the urgings of Netnokwa and the charms of a bold young Ojibwa woman, who asked him one day to share a pipe with her. This was highly unusual, Tanner noted, since most couples were brought together by their tribal elders and scarcely glanced at each other before marriage. After smoking with the young woman, he found himself dressing up as handsomely as he could and walking about the village, playing his reed flute to impress her.

He was in fact more eager to court her than marry her. When he arrived home one day and saw her seated inside his lodge, he hesitated to enter and join her, knowing that it would be taken as a commitment. But Netnokwa forced his hand. "Will you turn back from the door of the lodge," she asked, "and put this young woman to shame, who is in all respects better than you are? This affair has been of your seeking, and not of mine or hers." Stung by the reproach, Tanner sat down by his fiancée's side—and learned only later that Netnokwa had arranged matters with the young woman's parents while he was away and invited her into the lodge, confident that he would join her when pressed.

Neither this marriage nor a second one that Tanner entered into later proved happy. Although he was a diligent hunter who did all he could to provide for his children, he quarreled frequently with in-laws, who regarded him as an outsider and resented his denunciation of a medicine man they respected. Tanner's ambiguous position within the tribe resembled that of a fabled Ojibwa he had heard of, who accepted Christian baptism, only to discover after his death that he was welcome in neither the white man's paradise nor the Indian's.

Tanner's sense of isolation was compounded by the travails of the hunter's life and the toll that drinking took on him and his companions. At first, he avoided the rum and whiskey that traders commonly offered Indians for their furs, and tried to dissuade Netnokwa and others from "wasting all our peltries in purchasing what was not only useless, but hurtful and poisonous to us." But after a while, he too began to partake, much to Netnokwa's dismay. Even if he stayed sober at trading time, there was little he could do to keep his friends and kin from expending in a few days the proceeds of many months' labor. Afterward, they often had to purchase ammunition and provisions on credit in order to see their families through another winter.

After facing such challenges for nearly three decades, Tanner decided to return to the United States and find a place in white society, leaving his

An Ojibwa on snowshoes cradles his rifle in preparation for a winter deer hunt in this 19th-century photograph. Although firearms and snowshoes helped hunters of the lakes region get by through the course of the long, hard winter, they faced constant peril and prayed to protective spirits for survival.

children with his wife and her Ojibwa in-laws until he could get settled. Back in his native Kentucky, he was greeted warmly by his kin, who cut his long hair and dressed him as a white man. He felt uncomfortable in the stiff clothing, however, and found that it made him physically ill to sleep inside a house. He preferred to lie down at night in a "good place outside."

Ultimately he returned north to live once more in Indian country and seek employment there that would allow him to provide for his children. For the rest of his life, he moved from job to job, and several of his youngsters were raised by others. His travails in later years fulfilled the prophecy of the dream visitor, who had appeared to him one last time before he left for the United States. "Henceforth, you shall see me no more," the spirit proclaimed, "and that which remains before you, of your path, shall be full of briars and thorns."

His journey was indeed difficult. But the story of his years with the Ojibwa—which he related in 1830 to physician Edwin James, who committed it to writing under the title *The Falcon*—emerged as one of the most detailed portraits of life among Indians composed up to that time. Whatever differences Tanner may have had with Ojibwas over the years, he remained true to them in words and deeds, as he demonstrated shortly after returning to Canada, when he worked briefly as a trader for a fur company. He recognized that his profit would more than double if he offered Ojibwa hunters whiskey in payment. But after once trading with them in that way, he told his boss he would never do it again. "I had been so long among the Indians that many of them were personally my friends," he explained. "I was not willing to be myself active in spreading such poison among them." He owed as much to the Ojibwas, he added, for they regarded the Falcon as "one of their own."

Tanner was not the only white chronicler whose long sojourn among his adoptive people allowed him to speak for them. One witness who spent even longer than he did among Indians and testified with equal authority was Mary Jemison, who demonstrated that women as well as men could rise from captivity to a place of dignity within the tribe. Like James Smith, Jemison was taken prisoner in Pennsylvania during the French and Indian

War. In 1758, when she was about 15, six Shawnee warriors from the Ohio Valley, accompanied by four French soldiers, attacked her family's homestead near Gettysburg, plundered it for provisions, and made off with Mary, her father and mother, three of her siblings, and several neighbors who were visiting at the time.

For them as for many prisoners of the day, the journey into captivity was fraught with danger. Those who could not keep up with the warriors as they fled pursuit were sometimes put to death and scalped—a deed that both French and English authorities encouraged by offering their Indian allies bounties for enemy scalps. After a few days of hard journeying to evade search parties, the Shawnees placed moccasins on the feet of Mary and one of the neighbor's boys, signaling that they alone were to be spared, and separated them from the rest of the captives. A short time afterward, she saw the Shawnees scraping and stretching on hoops scalps that she recognized as those of her kin.

Within a few days, the war party reached Fort Duquesne, where James Smith had run the gantlet three years earlier. Jemison underwent no such ordeal. Instead, the Shawnees painted her face and hair red and

An Indian pours liquor from a keg while his Ojibwa and Assiniboin companions exhibit various degrees of intoxication in an 1820 painting by Swiss artist and traveler Peter Rindisbacher. Many traders eagerly plied the Indians with liquor, knowing that hunters under the influence would trade away a year's worth of pelts for what amounted to a few nights of revelry.

led her into the fort, where she met the two Seneca women who were to become her guardians and sisters. The Seneca were the westernmost nation of the Iroquois and had grown close to the French in recent years by frequenting their Great Lakes trading posts. Shawnees recognized Senecas as powerful allies in the ongoing war and honored them with gifts like that the warriors made when they offered Jemison to the two Seneca sisters, "to dispose of as they pleased."

The sisters welcomed Jemison because they had recently lost a brother in battle and longed to replenish their family. It mattered little that Jemison was a young woman and the relative she replaced a young man. If anything, she offered more to the family than a man would because Iroquois society was both matrilocal and matrilineal, meaning that any husband she took or children she bore would reside at her lodge and become part of her lineage, or kinship group.

Soon after Jemison arrived at the village of her new guardians in northern Pennsylvania, she was dressed as an Iroquois and took part in a remarkable observance that was part mourning ritual and part adoption ceremony. She did not yet know the Seneca language, but she later learned the meaning of the words spoken on such occasions and paraphrased the mourners. "He will never return!" the women said of their dead brother. "Friendless he died on the field of the slain, where his bones are yet lying unburied!" After heartily grieving his loss, however, they gave thanks that he had died bravely and that his soul had earned its reward: "With glory he fell, and his spirit went up to the land of his fathers in war! Then why do we mourn? With transports of joy they received him, and fed him, and clothed him, and welcomed him there! Oh friends, he is happy; then dry up your tears." Finally, they celebrated the arrival of a new sibling to comfort them: "In the place of our brother she stands in our tribe. With care we will guard her from trouble; and may she be happy till her spirit shall leave us."

By the conclusion of the ceremony, Jemison observed, her sisters had progressed from anguish to exultation: "Joy sparkled in their countenances, and they seemed to rejoice over me as over a long lost child." It was then that she received her Seneca name, Dehgewanus, meaning "Two Falling Voices," an apparent reference to her sisters and the deep consolation that muted their grief.

A few years after her adoption, a party of Delawares came to live with the Senecas, and Jemison's sisters arranged for her to marry a Delaware named Sheninjee, whom she found to be an "agreeable husband, and a

A bronze statue of Mary Jemison in Iroquois dress marks her burial place in Letchworth State Park, New York, overlooking the Genesee River valley, where she lived as a member of the Seneca Nation after being taken from her Pennsylvania home and adopted in her teens.

comfortable companion." She no longer pined to rejoin white society and had begun to view the world as her Indian relations did. She later recalled that her first child was born "at the time that the kernels of corn first appeared on the cob," marking the time by nature's calendar in tribal fashion. As dictated by custom, she went off to a birthing hut, attended by her two sisters. The child lived only two days, and Jemison fell deathly ill afterward, but she was well cared for and recovered "by the time the corn was ripe."

Jemison subsequently had a son whom she called Thomas Jemison—the first of several children she named after her white relatives, in keeping

HIOKATOO,

Mrs. Jemison's second husband, as he appeared when attired in his war dress. He died at Gardow Flats in 1811, at the advanced age of 103 years.

Mary Jemison's second husband, Hiokatoo, displays the outfit of a Seneca hunter-warrior in this illustration from Jemison's narrative. Hiokatoo was the father of four daughters and two sons by Jemison and endured, by her reckoning, to the ripe age of 103.

both with her own fond memories and with the Iroquois custom of tracing lineage through the mother. When Sheninjee died not long after Thomas was born, Jemison mourned for him, but the shock was lessened by the fact that she had remained with her Seneca mother and sisters and had their continuing support. They offered her "all the consolation in their power, and in a few months my grief wore off and I became contented."

Jemison later remarried and lived happily among the Senecas during the tranquil interlude before the American Revolution, which embroiled her people in further conflict. Allied with the English against the rebellious colonists—who were intent on eliminating barriers to white settlement in Indian territory recently proclaimed by English authorities—Senecas carried out raids on the Americans and were attacked by them in return. The reprisals devastated villages in western New York, where Senecas had expanded on their traditional corn-based horticulture by tending fruit groves and raising livestock.

Jemison recalled the devastating sweep by the forces of Major General John Sullivan through Iroquois country late in the war: "A part of our corn they burnt, and threw the remainder into the river. They burnt our houses, killed what few cattle and horses they could find, destroyed our fruit trees, and left nothing but the bare soil and timber." Desperate for subsistence, Jemison hired herself out to pick corn for two runaway slaves who had taken refuge in the area and pioneered a homestead. Not knowing that Jemison had long since been embraced by Senecas, one of them stood by with a loaded gun as Jemison worked, "fearing that I should get taken or injured by the Indians."

After the Revolution, Seneca chiefs assured Jemison that she was free to return to her white relatives if she so desired, but they insisted that her eldest son, who had matured to become a gifted warrior, stay behind. She was unwilling to leave Thomas and feared that if she managed to reach her relatives in Pennsylvania, they would treat her and her children "as enemies; or, at least with a degree of cold indifference, which I thought I could not endure." Gratified by her decision to remain, leaders of the tribe arranged in negotiations with white authorities for her to receive title to the land she and her children had been living on in recent years—a fertile tract along the Genesee River.

Some Senecas left the area for small reservations allotted to the tribe in New York. Others stayed on, as settlers began encroaching and claiming land or leasing it from titleholders like Jemison. Once again, as in her childhood, she found herself living on the frontier, where the interests of

whites and Indians collided. Increased contact with whites exposed more and more Senecas to the bane of alcohol and aggravated tensions between tribal traditionalists and accommodationists—with fatal consequences for Jemison's own family.

Thomas embodied the conflict between tribal values and those of white society. He enjoyed the respect that he received from Senecas for his prowess in battle, for example, but he "despised the cruelties that the warriors inflicted upon their subjugated enemies." Closer to home, he criticized his younger brother John—Jemison's son by her second husband—for taking two wives, claiming that such conduct was "inconsistent with the principles of good Indians." Thomas also denounced his brother in terms that were deeply rooted in tribal culture, insisting that John was a witch, a charge that Senecas sometimes leveled against people who acted in ways they regarded as unnatural or antisocial. Jemison herself confessed that "in fits of drunkenness," Thomas often threatened to take her life for having raised a witch. He once went so far as to menace her with a tomahawk, but in the end he himself was cut down by John, who shared his brother's weakness for liquor and murdered him during a drunken quarrel.

The family tragedy did not end there. John was acquitted by the tribal council, which excused him in light of the abuse he had received from Thomas over the years. Indeed, John was widely admired by Senecas for his powers as a healer and visionary. He practiced as a doctor in tribal fash-

This rough-hewn cabin, built by Mary Jemison for her daughter Nancy in 1800, was typical of the shelters then occupied by whites and Indians alike in western New York. The cabin was moved from its original location to Mary Jemison's grave site.

ion by administering "roots and herbs, which he gathered in the forests, and other places where they had been planted by the hand of nature." Jemison later learned that John had dreamed of murdering Thomas before the fact and had been advised by a fellow medicine man to "govern his temper, and avoid any quarrel which in future he might see arising." Unfortunately, he lost his self-control under the influence of alcohol, and he later became embroiled in another drunken clash that claimed the life of Jemison's youngest and dearest son, Jesse, who was intensely proud of his white ancestry and had long been at odds with John. In the end, John himself met a violent end at the hands of two unrelated Senecas—an end he foresaw in a vision just days before the attack occurred.

Jemison spent the rest of her life on the land granted to her, haunted by the strife that had convulsed her family but determined to do well by her surviving children. Some Senecas whispered that she was a "great witch," but others denied it, and no harm came to her. Senecas had some reason to regard her as an outsider, for she never cast off her former identity entirely—any more than John Tanner did. Both were torn at times between the tribal values they adopted and the standards of white society. Neither adoption nor intermarriage could erase that conflict, for outsiders who entered tribal circles brought opposing attitudes with them, introducing tensions that persisted over decades and endured from one generation to the next.

Even when they were telling of lingering differences with their adoptive people, however, chroniclers like Jemison and Tanner enlightened whites, who learned of native cultures that were rich and strong enough to rival their own. A fuller understanding of those societies would come later, from observers of a different breed, who ventured gladly among Indians and documented their traditions at length. But witnesses who were forced into tribal circles and found a measure of fulfillment there communicated something fundamental upon which all cultural understanding depended—respect for Native Americans and their powers. ✛

This salt container was tightly woven from cornhusks by one of Mary Jemison's contemporaries among the Iroquois, who made the most of their corn harvests by putting every part of the plant to use.

TREASURES FROM NATIVE AMERICA

Europeans who ventured to the New World chronicled their encounters with Indians for posterity not only by keeping journals but also by collecting tribal artifacts of timeless beauty. For early explorers, such treasures served to authenticate their reports of exotic new lands and peoples and were sometimes presented as gifts to royal sponsors. As exploration gave way to colonization, missionaries, traders, and officials sent Indian artifacts to their superiors in Europe or built up their own "cabinets," or collections of tribal handiwork, as mementos of their travels and experiences. By the 19th century, Europeans were organizing formal scientific expeditions to collect Native American artifacts for study and exhibition. Whether gathered as a result of exploration, colonization, or scientific inquiry, some of the finest of these works ended up in museums across Europe, where future generations could discover anew the artistry and ingenuity of the first Americans.

Nootka men dance in front of Spanish tents at Friendly Cove on Vancouver Island as other tribal members look on from their canoes in a drawing by Tomás de Suria, an artist who accompanied the explorer Alejandro Malaspina on his reconnaissance of America's Northwest Coast in the 1790s. Many of the Indians can be seen wearing caps like the Nootka whaler's hat below, woven of spruce root and collected by Malaspina.

Heirlooms of the Northwest Coast

Malaspina's expedition, commissioned by Spain's King Carlos IV in 1790, was in part an effort to protect and extend the Spanish empire. But it also reflected a growing scientific curiosity about native peoples during the Enlightenment. Long after the Spanish empire crumbled, Malaspina's cultural finds, including the Tlingit treasures shown here, endured in a collection at Madrid's Museo de América.

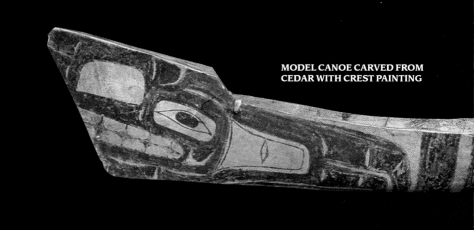

MODEL CANOE CARVED FROM CEDAR WITH CREST PAINTING

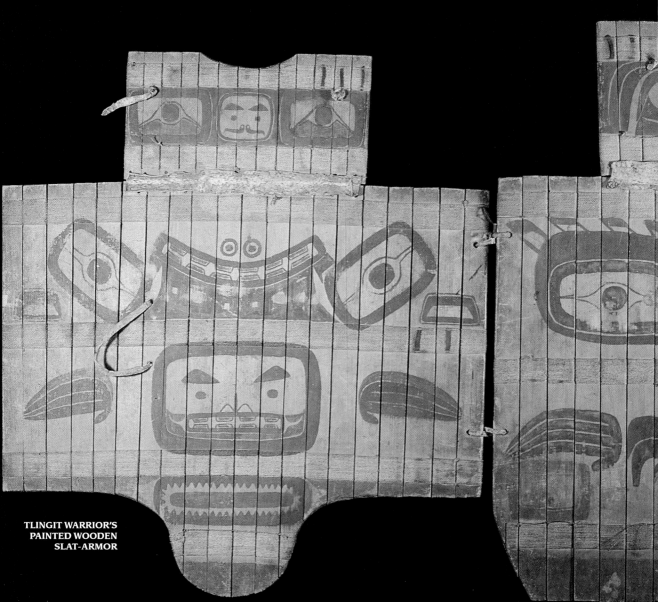

TLINGIT WARRIOR'S PAINTED WOODEN SLAT-ARMOR

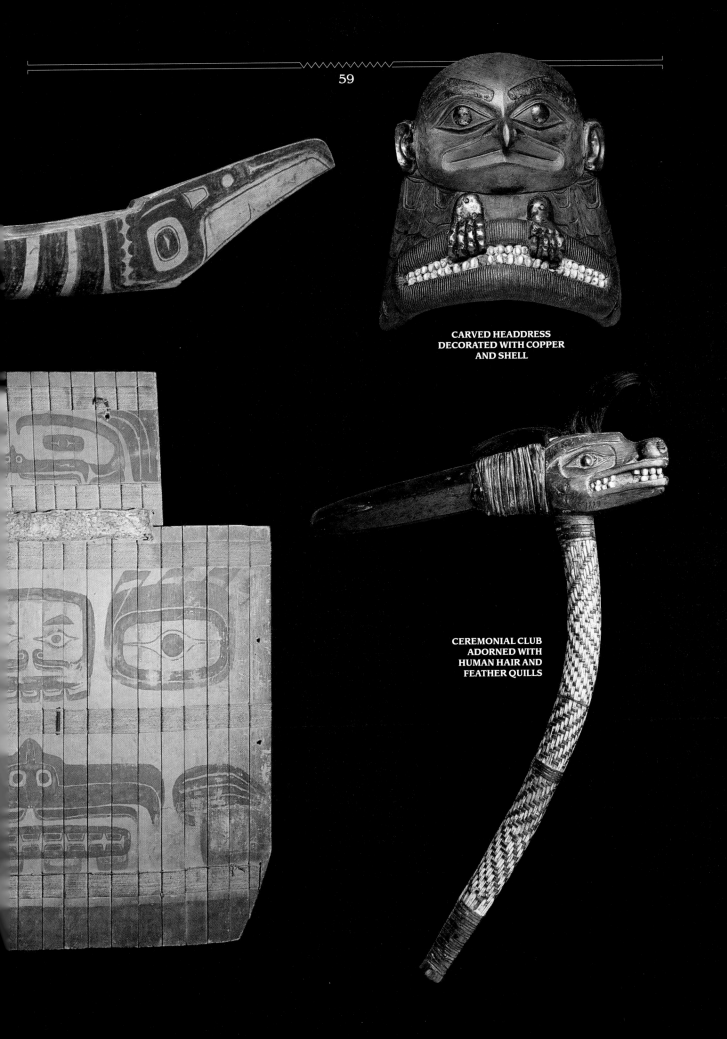

**CARVED HEADDRESS
DECORATED WITH COPPER
AND SHELL**

**CEREMONIAL CLUB
ADORNED WITH
HUMAN HAIR AND
FEATHER QUILLS**

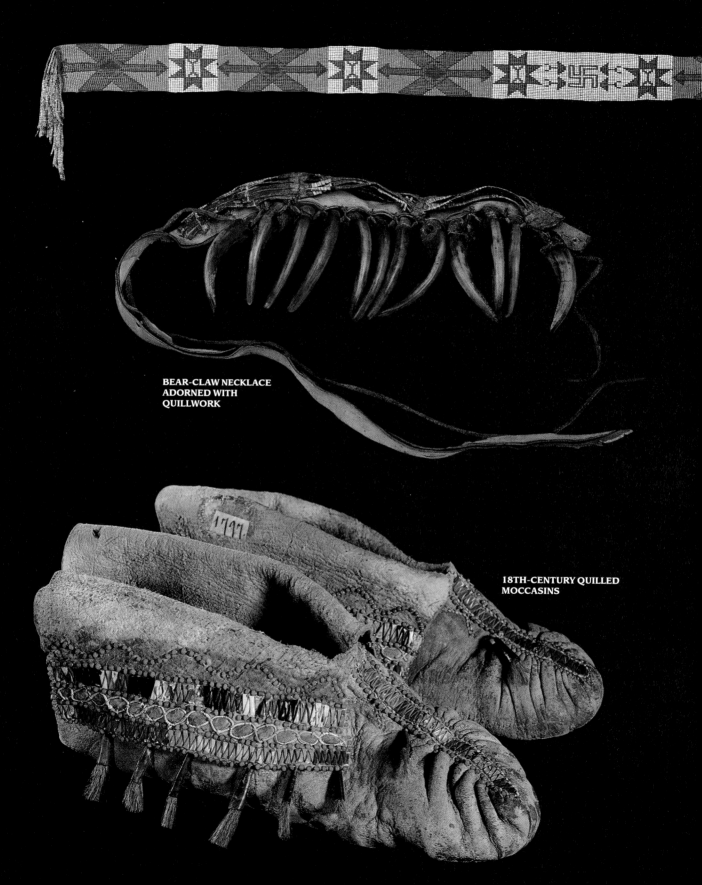

BEAR-CLAW NECKLACE
ADORNED WITH
QUILLWORK

18TH-CENTURY QUILLED
MOCCASINS

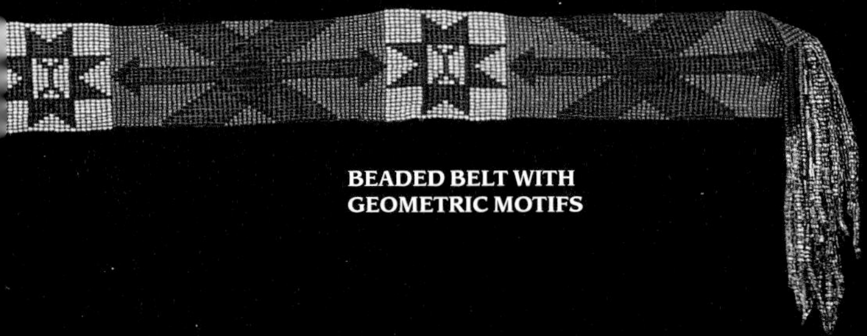

BEADED BELT WITH
GEOMETRIC MOTIFS

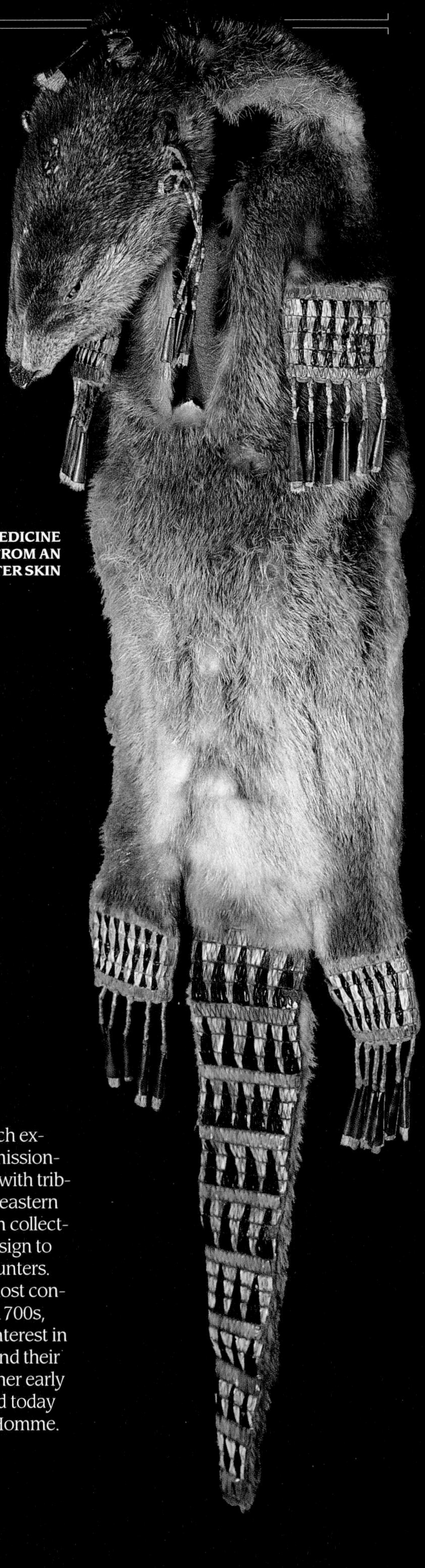

OJIBWA MEDICINE
BAG MADE FROM AN
OTTER SKIN

KNIFE-CASE NECKLACE
FROM THE GREAT
LAKES AREA

KEEPSAKES OF NEW FRANCE

From the 1500s, French explorers, traders, and missionaries established ties with tribal groups in the northeastern
woodlands and began collecting items of native design to
document their encounters.
Although the French lost control of Canada in the 1700s,
they maintained an interest in
the region's Indians and their
culture. These and other early
artifacts are preserved today
in Paris's Musée de l'Homme.

CARVED PIPE
BOWL IN THE SHAPE
OF A WAR CLUB

Prizes of an Irish Soldier

Among the avid collectors on the frontier of British North America in the early 1800s was Jasper Grant, an Irishman who served as a military officer in the Great Lakes region. A keen eye and an appreciation for Indians and their works enabled him to assemble a remarkable cabinet of "curiosities"—handcrafted objects from various Great Lakes tribes allied with the British at the time. Grant bequeathed his collection to his grandson, who donated it to the National Museum of Ireland in Dublin.

EMBROIDERED BELT POUCH

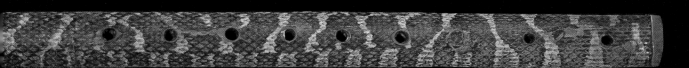

**COURTING FLUTE COVERED WITH
THE SKIN OF A WATER SNAKE**

**WOVEN BAG WITH THUNDER-
BIRD AND LIGHTNING DESIGNS**

**QUILLED POUCH
DECORATED WITH
METAL BANGLES**

A COLLECTION FROM THE PLAINS

In 1823 Friedrich Paul Wilhelm, the duke of Württemberg, forsook a military career in his native land in order to canvass the American West for Indian artifacts. Among tribes such as the Sioux, he observed, the art of decorating useful objects had "advanced to a high degree of perfection." He documented that artistry by assembling an outstanding collection of Prairie and Plains Indian handiwork, much of which is housed today in the Linden-Museum in Stuttgart, Germany.

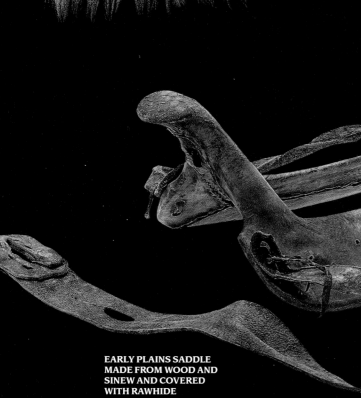

**EARLY PLAINS SADDLE
MADE FROM WOOD AND
SINEW AND COVERED
WITH RAWHIDE**

EARLY-19TH-CENTURY
OMAHA BOW CASE,
ARROWS, AND QUIVER

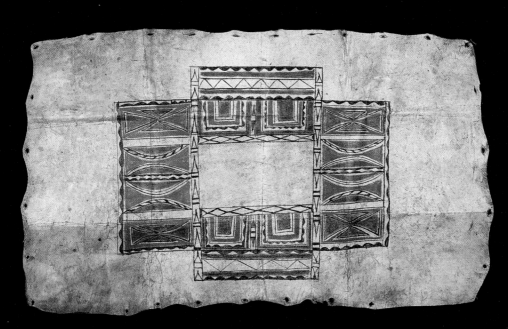

DAKOTA RAWHIDE PARFLECHE,
OR CONTAINER, UNFOLDED

66

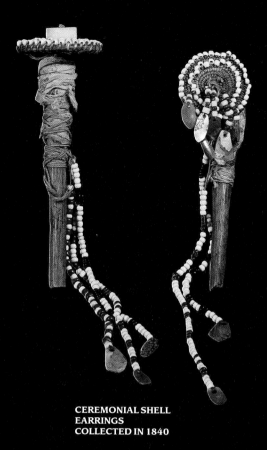

CEREMONIAL SHELL
EARRINGS
COLLECTED IN 1840

BELT WOVEN WITH
NATIVE GRASSES
AND FEATHERS

A RUSSIAN TROVE FROM CALIFORNIA

Before the Russians abandoned their North American claims with the sale of Alaska to the United States in 1867, they amassed a wealth of Indian items along the Pacific coast as traders and scientific collectors. In 1839 Ivan Gavrilovich Voznesenski was dispatched from Saint Petersburg to California to gather tribal artifacts for display in Russia. Scores of Native American creations collected by Voznesenski continue to dazzle visitors to museums such as the Kunstkamera in Saint Petersburg.

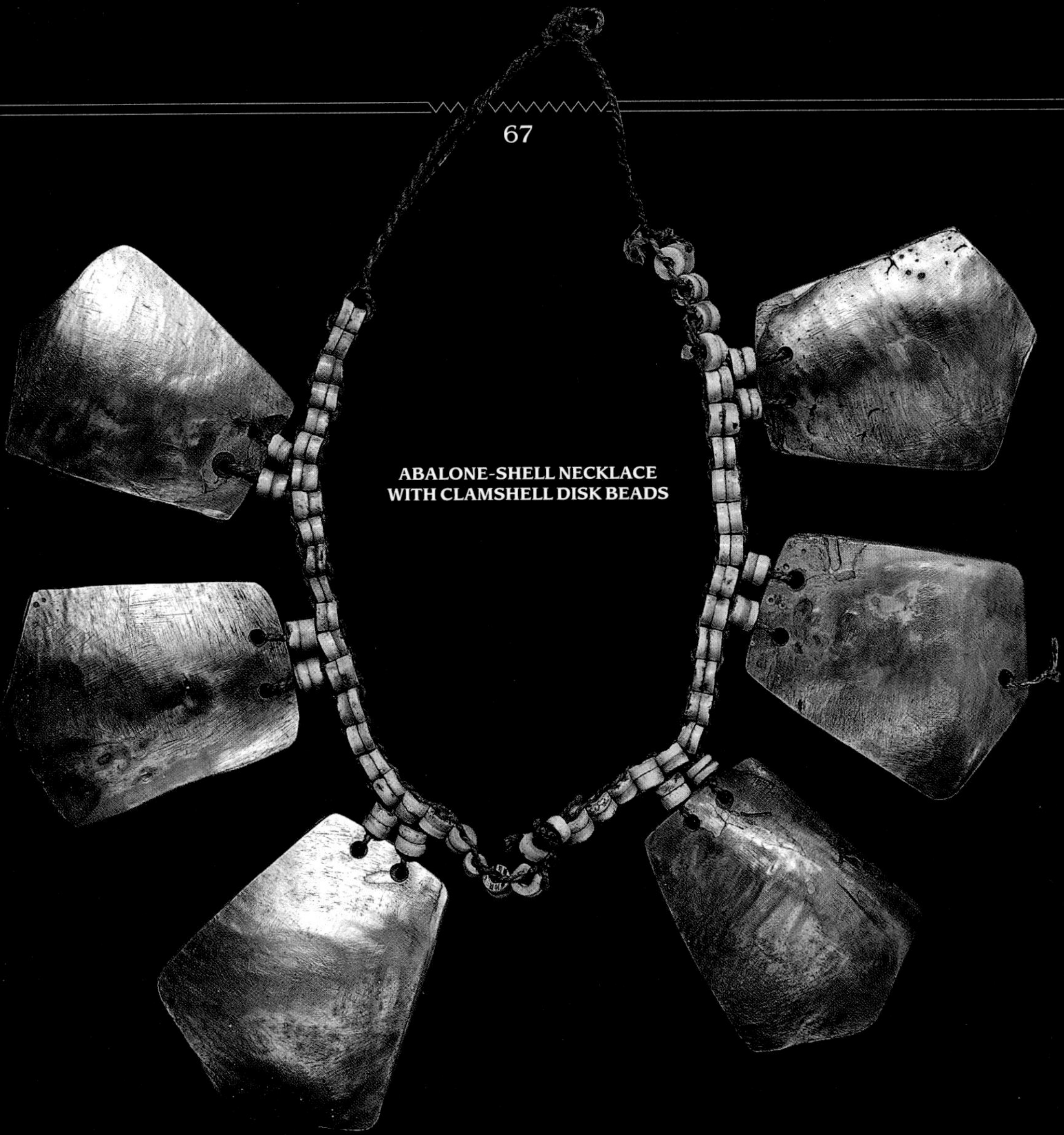

ABALONE-SHELL NECKLACE
WITH CLAMSHELL DISK BEADS

BASKET ORNAMENTED
WITH SHELLS
AND TRADE BEADS

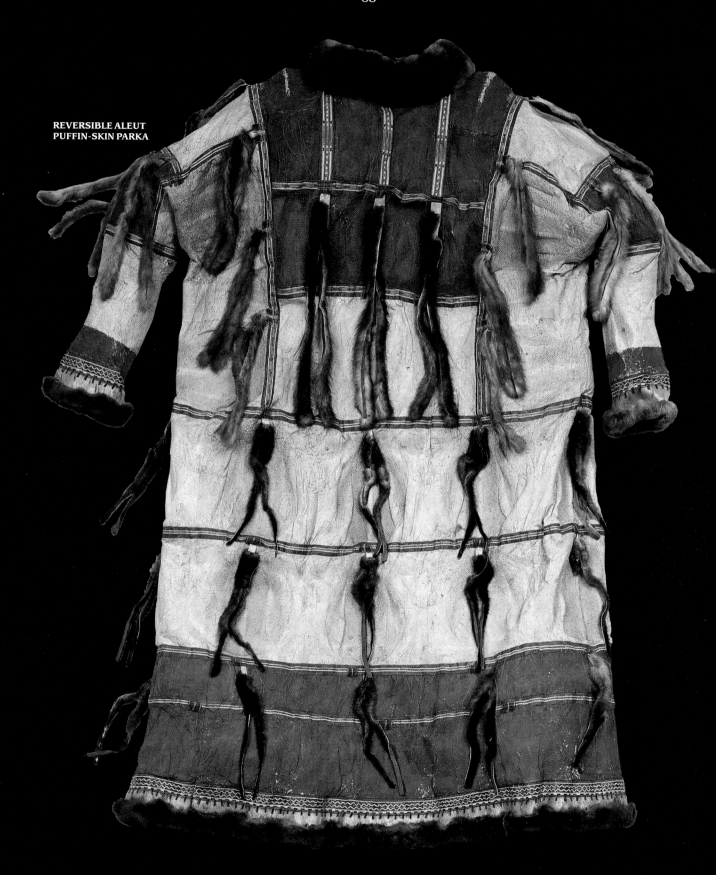

**REVERSIBLE ALEUT
PUFFIN-SKIN PARKA**

ALEUT WOODEN HUNT-
ING HAT DECORATED
WITH WALRUS IVORY
AND WHISKERS

ARCTIC MASTERWORKS

In 1817 an 18-year-old Finn
by the name of Adolf Etholén
traveled to Alaska, where he
served the Russian colony
diligently as an administrator
for nearly three decades, rising to become its highest offi-
cial. During that time, Etholén
avidly collected hundreds of
marvelous artifacts from
Aleuts of Alaska's southern
coast and other native peoples living to the north—treasures that are preserved today
at the National Museum of
Finland in Helsinki.

ESKIMO-CARVED SEA
OTTER EFFIGY ADORNED
WITH SQUIRREL AND
CARIBOU HAIR

ALEUT BOX CARVED FROM
MAMMOTH IVORY AND DECORATED
WITH SEAL HAIR

2

PORTRAYING THE PEOPLE

Bundled against the frigid winds, Mandan Indians carry firewood across the frozen Missouri River to their village atop the far bluff in a scene depicted by visiting Swiss artist Karl Bodmer in the 1830s. The Lewis and Clark expedition wintered here from November 1804 to April 1805 and established close ties with the Mandan; the area later became the site of an American trading post, Fort Clark (background, left).

By the last day of November 1804, winter had tightened its grip on Mandan country. Snow cloaked the bluffs along the Missouri River, and thick clots of ice drifted downstream with the current. In the bleak dawn light, smoke rose from the rooftops of starkly contrasting settlements on either side of the Missouri. To the west lay the Mandan village of Mitutanka, a companionable cluster of mound-shaped, earth-covered lodges that mimicked the surrounding prairie, with its low ridges and swales. To the east rose an isolated compound of wooden huts, freshly built by a group of explorers led by Captains Meriwether Lewis and William Clark. Their party, known as the Corps of Discovery, had christened the camp Fort Mandan for the host tribe that graciously allowed them to pass the winter there in what would come to be known as North Dakota.

Shortly after sunrise, a man from Mitutanka came down to the west bank and called out to the occupants of the fort, several of whom crossed the icy river in a dugout canoe and returned with the messenger. Speaking through an interpreter, he informed the explorers that a Mandan hunting party had been ambushed not far from the village by a combined force of Sioux and Arikara warriors, who had claimed the life of one hunter, wounded two others, and made off with some horses.

Such raids were uncommon in winter, but the identity of the attackers came as no surprise to the Mandan. They had long been at odds with the Arikara—who lived along the Missouri to the south—and with the powerful Lakota Sioux, who pursued buffalo on the Plains and used the surplus meat and hides they garnered to trade with whites for weapons and tools and with village-dwelling tribes along the Missouri for crops. The Mandan themselves sometimes hosted Sioux and Arikara traders and bartered with them, but the hostilities persisted. Mandan villagers expected such assaults and were prepared to respond—when the time was right. Winter was not the best season for revenge. The messenger visited Fort Mandan to alert the explorers to danger, not to enlist their support for swift reprisals.

For Lewis and Clark, however, the raid came as a challenge and demanded an immediate response. Six months earlier, they had departed

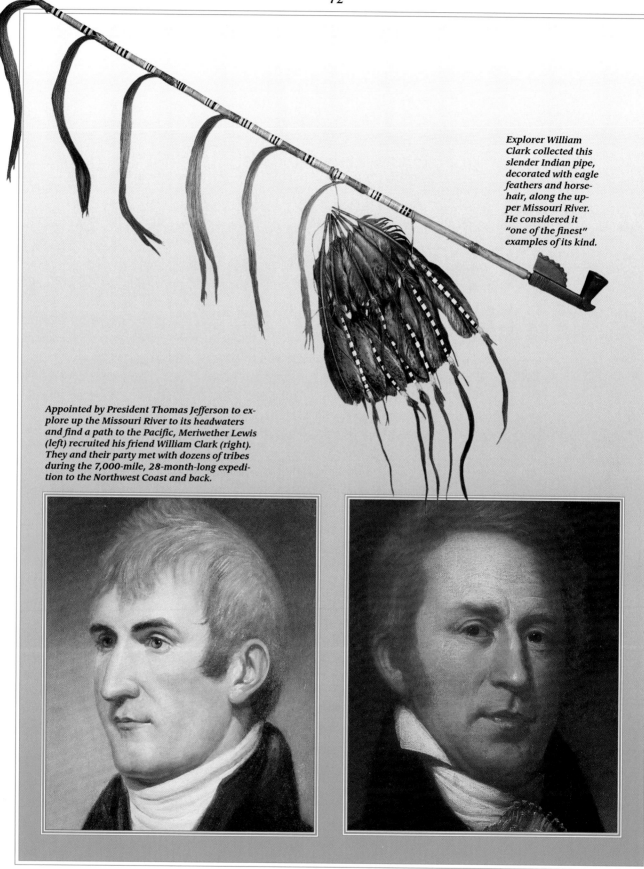

Explorer William Clark collected this slender Indian pipe, decorated with eagle feathers and horsehair, along the upper Missouri River. He considered it "one of the finest" examples of its kind.

Appointed by President Thomas Jefferson to explore up the Missouri River to its headwaters and find a path to the Pacific, Meriwether Lewis (left) recruited his friend William Clark (right). They and their party met with dozens of tribes during the 7,000-mile, 28-month-long expedition to the Northwest Coast and back.

Saint Louis and headed up the Missouri on their pathfinding journey—a venture that was partly scientific in nature and partly diplomatic. Through the Louisiana Purchase, the United States had acquired from France claims to a vast area west of the Mississippi River. The diplomatic mission of Lewis and Clark was to proclaim American sovereignty to tribes of the upper Missouri and the Pacific Northwest and to persuade those groups to become peaceful members of a prospective American trade network.

In September, however, before reaching Mandan country, the explorers had encountered Lakota chiefs in present-day South Dakota who seemed distinctly unimpressed with American might. They came away convinced that the Sioux would not soon be won over and that American traders would have to rely on more settled tribes, including the Arikara—whom Lewis and Clark visited in October—the Mandan, and the Hidatsa, who lived just north of their Mandan allies. Ignoring the complexities of intertribal relations, Lewis and Clark blamed the Sioux for setting the Arikara against the Mandan and hoped that all three Missouri River tribes would rally around the Americans if they responded forcefully to Sioux provocation.

Clark, who had more experience than Lewis in dealing with Indians on the frontier, took charge of the punitive expedition. He mustered a force of two dozen armed men and led them across the Missouri by boat and through the snow to Mitutanka. The Mandan were "not expecting to receive such strong aid in so short a time," Clark wrote in his journal afterward, and they were alarmed by the "formidable appearance of my party." Clark tried to reassure them, explaining that he was there to "meet the army of Sioux and chastise them for taking the blood of our dutiful children," as he referred to the Mandan.

In dealings with the explorers, the Mandan went along with such language and addressed the Americans as "fathers," perhaps because in their culture fathers would offer their children counsel rather than give them commands. By no means did the Mandan feel obliged to obey the Americans or follow their lead. They soon made it clear to Clark that they regarded his proposed expedition as ill conceived. As always, however, they expressed themselves with great tact. A spokesman named Oheenaw, a Cheyenne who had been adopted into the tribe, first thanked Clark for coming to their aid. He placed part of the blame on the Mandan themselves, who were so distracted by American talk of peace on the Missouri that some of them "carelessly went out to hunt in small parties" and exposed themselves to ambush. The real culprits, Oheenaw insisted, were the Arikara, who were "liars and bad men" and needed no prodding from

the Sioux to disturb the peace. Oheenaw then made a counterproposal: "My father, the snow is deep and it is cold; our horses cannot travel through the plains; those people who have spilt our blood have gone back. If you will go with us in the spring after the snow goes off, we will raise the warriors of all the towns and nations around about us, and go with you."

With a few choice words, Oheenaw had punctured the diplomatic illusions of the Americans. Chastising the Sioux would not resolve the conflict between the Mandan and the Arikara or other longstanding tribal disputes in the region. Furthermore, no party that was merely passing through the country could hope to alter intertribal relations in any lasting way. By suggesting that the reprisals be postponed until spring—by which time the restless Americans would be on their way—Oheenaw was gently reminding them that they should not meddle in delicate and dangerous matters unless they planned to remain in the area and reckon with the consequences of their actions. Such was the rhetorical skill of Oheenaw and his fellow chiefs that they managed to deflect the Americans from folly without making them feel foolish. Clark abandoned his plans and led his men back to the safety of the fort. Yet he did so with soothing assurances from the Mandan that they valued his show of support and that they would now "wipe away their tears, and rejoice in their father's protection."

Although Clark's foray seemingly accomplished little, such lessons in tribal diplomacy proved highly instructive, both for the explorers themselves and for those who subsequently read their accounts. Indeed, one of the chief missions of Lewis and Clark was to serve as chroniclers. As requested by President Thomas Jefferson, they kept a careful record of

In a drawing illustrating the account of expedition member Patrick Gass, Lewis addresses a group of Indians along the Missouri. Speaking through interpreters, Lewis and Clark routinely greeted tribespeople in the name of the president, whom the explorers referred to as the Great Chief or Great Father.

their dealings with Indians, preserving for posterity the words of shrewd chiefs like Oheenaw and adding significantly to the fund of knowledge about the region's tribes.

Jefferson had long been interested in the customs of American Indians, both in his native Virginia and in more remote areas. Since childhood, he wrote, he had learned all he could about Indians "and acquired impressions of attachment and commiseration for them which have never been obliterated." In that curiosity and "commiseration," the president embodied the spirit of the Enlightenment, an intellectual movement nurtured in Europe that helped shape the democratic ideals of Jefferson and other founders of the American republic. Among their cherished principles was faith in the power of reason to overcome intolerance and oppression. Jefferson believed that tribal peoples should be studied, not simply dismissed or condemned. From such study would come the knowledge and respect that diplomats, traders, and military men needed to avert conflict with Indians and reconcile them to the demands of an expanding American nation. Like most of his contemporaries, Jefferson assumed that Indians would ultimately have to adopt the ways of white Americans or face extinction. But he believed that they could be won over only by people who understood their traditions and honored their principles.

The very idea that tribal cultures were worth studying on their own terms was fairly recent. Since the time of Columbus, Europeans had been observing Indian lifeways through the distorting lens of their own beliefs. Early Jesuit missionaries in Canada, for example, honored the scholarly tradition of their order by learning the languages of the tribes they lived among and by composing detailed "relations," or reports, on tribal customs. Yet the priests dismissed sacred Indian ceremonies as devil worship and regarded other tribal traditions as mere savagery. It took a Jesuit of a later era—one touched by the spirit of the Enlightenment—to reinterpret those reports in light of his own telling observations. In 1724 Father Joseph-François Lafitau, who had served as a missionary to the Caughnawaga near Montreal and pored over the reports of earlier Jesuits, dared to take issue with the assumptions of his predecessors. "I have seen with great distress," he wrote, "in the greater part of the *Relations* that those who have written of the customs of barbarous peoples have represented them to us as persons possessing no feeling whatever for religion, no knowledge of the divinity, no objects of worship; as peoples who have neither laws, nor foreign policy, nor form of government; as persons, in a word, who could claim nothing human but their shape."

Lafitau compared the culture of American Indians with that of pagans in ancient times and demonstrated that Indians, like the pagans, had their own religions, rules, and forms of government. He rejected the claims of earlier priests and travelers who stated that "only the men among the Indians are really free and that the women are only their slaves." Among the Iroquois, Lafitau pointed out, women wielded great power: "In them resides all the real authority: the lands, fields, and all their harvest belong to them; they are the souls of the councils, the arbiters of peace and war."

Such keen insights marked the dawn of modern ethnography—a term of Greek origin meaning simply the "description of people." As Lafitau demonstrated, it took more than careful observation to make sense of an unfamiliar culture. The observer needed sympathy and imagination to enter into the lives of those he was studying and to see the world as they did. In time, ethnography would become the province of professionals, known today as anthropologists. But its early practitioners were discerning witnesses from all walks of life. Among those who first helped convey the views of American Indians to the public at large were missionaries like Lafitau, artists like George Catlin, and explorers and soldiers like Lewis and Clark.

Lewis and Clark acted as ethnographers by documenting their encounters with Indians in various ways. They collected tribal goods and artifacts, including tools, hide paintings, and bean seeds that Jefferson later planted experimentally at his Monticello estate. They compiled maps, relying in part on interviews with Indians, who had long drawn their own charts of trails and terrain. But above all, the explorers kept detailed journals, in compliance with Jefferson's wish that this would be an important "literary expedition," whose diaries would contribute significantly to the annals of ethnography.

Although Lewis and Clark amassed information about many tribes during their epic journey to the Pacific and back, they learned most about the Mandan and their Hidatsa neighbors. Held captive by the Dakota winter, the party of some 30 men—including several French traders and interpreters along with American recruits—had no choice but to linger among their hosts. They camped at Fort Mandan for more than five months and entered into a complex and revealing relationship with the surrounding Indians.

Throughout their stay, they traded with the villagers, offering them glass beads, sewing needles, and metal implements in exchange for corn and other crops that tribeswomen harvested from their gardens and stored in underground caches. The Mandan tried to monopolize that trade by

Lewis and Clark shipped this buffalo hide, depicting a battle between the Mandan and their Sioux rivals, from Fort Mandan to President Jefferson in early 1805. Lewis and Clark secured such gifts from Indians by offering them various items, including peace medals bearing Jefferson's image.

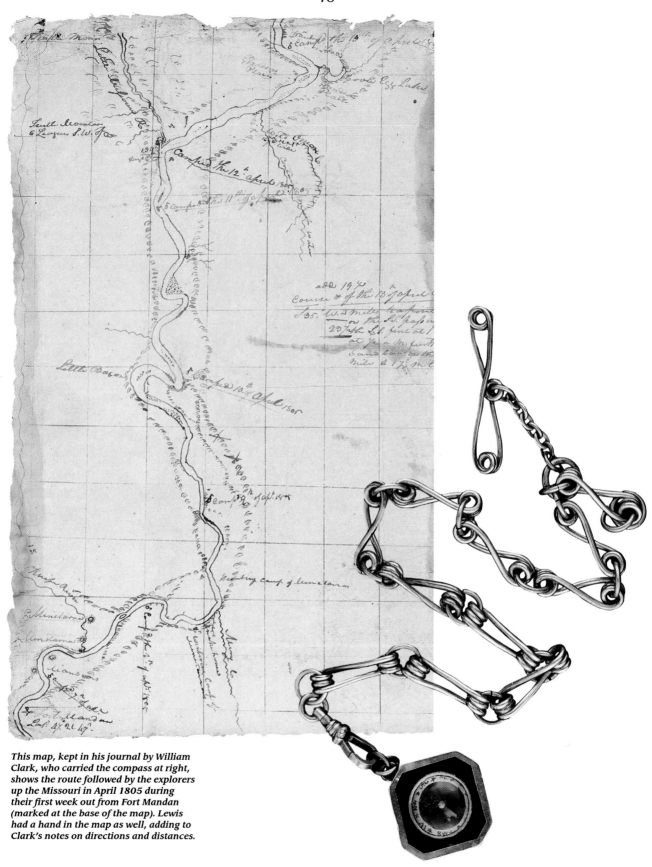

This map, kept in his journal by William Clark, who carried the compass at right, shows the route followed by the explorers up the Missouri in April 1805 during their first week out from Fort Mandan (marked at the base of the map). Lewis had a hand in the map as well, adding to Clark's notes on directions and distances.

During their winter at Fort Mandan, the explorers obtained corn from surrounding Indians by offering them the services of the party's blacksmith, who repaired and crafted battle-axes like the one sketched here in Lewis's journal. Lewis noted that the blades were sometimes perforated with holes "by way of ornament."

telling the Hidatsa—whose villages lay several miles upstream from Fort Mandan—that the whites might attack them if they approached the camp. Lewis and Clark countered those charges by paying calls on Hidatsa chiefs and urging them to visit. But the explorers met resentments. When Lewis called at the lodge of one Hidatsa leader, he was told the chief was "not at home," a form of rejection Lewis was surprised to encounter among Indians. Try as they might, the explorers could not achieve the same rapport with the Hidatsa as with the Mandan. Their very presence had stirred up a lingering rivalry between the two tribes.

As the explorers grew dependent on the Mandan for provisions and information, they ceased to be mere observers or mediators and became actively involved in the tribal culture and economy. At times, men from the fort went out with Indian hunting parties and stalked buffalo or antelope, but game was scarce. To encourage villagers to part with their stored crops, the explorers offered them the services of their blacksmith in exchange. At first, the smith simply mended or sharpened iron tools for the Indians, but when that business slackened, he began to repair battle-axes and make new ones. To keep the forge blazing, Lewis and Clark dispatched men from the camp to cut timber for the kiln. Despite their mandate to promote peace, they found that dealing in battle-axes was the "only means by which we procure corn." The coveted weapons circulated far and wide among Indians. A year later, members of the party spotted axes from Fort Mandan at a Nez Perce village in the Northwest.

Men at Fort Mandan became caught up in the life of the tribe in a more immediate way as well—through sexual encounters with women of the nearby villages. Earlier in the journey, Lewis and Clark had confounded Lakota chiefs by rejecting their offers of women as consorts. Clark noted that he twice turned down such invitations, despite urgings from the chiefs that he accept "and not despise them." As expedition leaders, Lewis and Clark may have felt obliged to avoid sexual entanglements, but they imposed no such restrictions on their men when the party later visited the Arikara and camped near the Mandan.

Sometimes men of the corps offered gifts for sexual favors, but the women they sought out were attracted less by material goods than by the medicine, or spirit power, they attributed to men of other races, whether white or black. Clark's servant, York, for example, was of African descent, and he was looked upon with awe; on one occasion, he slept with an Arikara woman at the invitation of her husband. Tribespeople welcomed such contact for the same reason they adopted members of other groups—the urge to strengthen the band by incorporating the powers of outsiders. To that end, men from the fort were invited to take part in a Mandan buffalo-hunting ritual. During the ceremony, younger, less experienced hunters traditionally offered their wives to older males as a way of obtaining some of their skill and success. According to Pierre-Antoine Tabeau, a French trader in the area, Mandans extended the sexual invitation to the visitors as well, in the hope of acquiring their medicine and attracting elusive herds of buffalo. In Tabeau's words, the visitors gladly accepted the offer and proved "untiringly zealous in attracting the cow."

In this and other ways, the visitors lost their detachment and became part of the ongoing drama, much to the delight of their hosts. The Mandan and Hidatsa loved to watch men from the fort dance jigs to the accompaniment of fiddle, tambourine, and other exotic instruments. On New Year's Day, 1805, more than a dozen men from the camp visited Mitutanka, fired their guns in the air, and pranced about for the villagers, who repaid them with gifts of buffalo robes and corn.

Such interplay helped erode the barriers between the two sides and allowed Lewis and Clark to catch glimpses of the heart of the culture. Clark related a Mandan origin story that told of an underground village from which their ancient ancestors emerged by means of a grapevine: "Some of the most adventurous climbed up the vine and were delighted with the sight of the earth, which they found covered with buffalo and rich with every kind of fruits. Returning with the grapes they had gathered, their countrymen were so pleased with the taste of them that the whole nation resolved to leave their dull residence for the charms of the upper region. Men, women, and children ascended by means of the vine; but when about half the nation had reached the surface of the earth, a corpulent woman who was clambering up the vine broke it with her weight, and closed upon herself and the rest of the nation the light of the sun." Those dwelling on the face of the earth said that when they died they would return to the village below to reside among their forebears. Such legends helped to explain the profound attachment of the Mandan and other tribes to their home territory, the land of their origin and destiny.

Further insights into Mandan beliefs would have to await the arrival of future visitors. By March, the ice was breaking up on the Missouri, and the

Artist George Catlin, who visited the Mandan in the summer of 1832, portrayed himself here beside Chief Mahtotohpa (Four Bears), who invited him for a feast that included buffalo ribs and turnip-flour pudding. Catlin noted that the chief did not dine with him but sat politely nearby, "ready to wait upon" his guest, if need be.

explorers were caulking their boats and preparing to move on. They departed on April 7, continuing up the Missouri and taking with them as a guide a young Shoshone woman named Sacajawea, who had been captured by Hidatsas during a raid and acquired as a wife by a French Canadian trader who joined the expedition as an interpreter.

The Corps of Discovery left behind a mixed legacy at their winter camp. Their visit foretold an era of increased contact with whites for the Mandan and Hidatsa, whose homeland would soon become the site of an American trading post called Fort Clark. Such commerce increased the risk that the two tribes would again be devastated by disease, as they had been by smallpox more than two decades before Lewis and Clark arrived. But before that calamity recurred, the Mandan and Hidatsa would profit by the growing trade and flourish, as documented by gifted observers who followed in the path of Lewis and Clark and beheld these proud tribal cultures in full bloom.

In the summer of 1832, George Catlin arrived at Fort Clark to compose another chapter in his remarkable pictorial chronicle of America's Indians. Born in Pennsylvania in 1796, Catlin came of age at a time when most eastern tribes were already confined to reservations. His mother could

Mahtoheha (Old Bear), the leading Mandan shaman, sang a medicine song while Catlin painted this portrait of him in all his finery, holding his pipes adorned with eagle feathers. Afterward, the shaman was so taken with the portrait that he lay "for hours together, day after day," Catlin wrote, "gazing intently upon it."

remember when Indians had resisted white intrusions—she herself had been taken captive briefly by a war party in 1778. But to young Catlin, Indians were a source of fascination rather than fear. Trained as a lawyer, he abandoned that career in the 1820s to try his hand at portraiture in Philadelphia, where he was deeply impressed with a delegation of Indian chiefs who passed through on their way to Washington, D.C., and met the gaze of curious onlookers "in silent and stoic dignity," as he put it. That encounter quickened his resolve to visit as many tribes as he could and bring home "faithful portraits of their principal personages, and full notes of their character and history." After refining his craft in upstate New York, where he portrayed several Iroquois leaders, he departed in 1830 for Saint Louis. There he met William Clark—now U.S. superintendent of Indian affairs—and embarked with Clark's support on a campaign to capture on canvas every western tribe within reach.

At Fort Clark, Catlin met Mandans and Hidatsas who were used to dealing with white men. But they had never been visited by a portrait painter, and they feared Catlin's medicine. In their experience, to portray something was to summon its spirit and gain control over it, as tribal artists did when they depicted the buffalo they stalked or the enemies they pursued. Thus villagers were at first reluctant to place themselves under Catlin's power. After some effort, he persuaded a Mandan chief called Mahtotohpa, or Mató-Tópe (Four Bears), and another tribal leader to sit for him at Fort Clark. When the portraits were displayed, villagers warned that Catlin had robbed his subjects of part of their "existence" and transferred it to the picture. Chiefs met in council and debated whether to banish the artist.

James Kipp, an agent at Fort Clark, assured the chiefs that Catlin's portraits were meant to honor those depicted. Mandan warriors sometimes celebrated their own feats or those of esteemed ancestors in paintings, and the chiefs concluded that Catlin's motives were similarly respectful. They embraced him as a medicine man by sacrificing a dog and hanging the carcass over the door of his studio and presenting him with a *sheshequoi*—a medicine staff and rattle adorned with bats' wings and grizzly bear claws.

Afterward, many prominent Mandans posed for Tehopenee Washee, or Great Medicine White Man, as they called Catlin. But his newfound popularity vexed the leading shaman Mahtoheha (Old Bear). As Catlin related, the shaman warned those who agreed to be portrayed that they were "fools and would soon die . . . materially affecting thereby my popularity." Catlin invited Mahtoheha to his studio and assured him that he had been informed of his importance and had been practicing his hand on others so

that he could do justice to the great shaman on canvas. At that, Mahtoheha shook Catlin's hand and shared a pipe with him. "I am glad that my people have told you who I am," he declared. "I will go to my wigwam and eat, and in a little while I will come, and you may go to work." Several hours later, he returned to pose, "bedaubed and streaked with paints of various colors . . . with medicine pipes in his hands and foxtails attached to his heels."

Once the portrait was completed to Mahtoheha's satisfaction, he became a firm ally of Catlin's. He later invited the artist to observe the tribe's most sacred ceremony, the Okipa. Similar in nature to the Sun Dances performed by other Plains tribes, the ritual was conducted annually by the Mandan in midsummer to seek blessings from the Great Spirit and to ward off evil. The ceremony opened with the dramatic arrival of Mahtoheha, impersonating the tribal hero First Man, who according to legend had escaped a great flood in ancient times by climbing the mountains to the west, where he survived to replenish the world. First Man approached the village from the west, coated with white clay and garbed in white wolf skins. After being greeted with acclaim, he opened the medicine lodge in the center of the village and warned the people that unless they made the proper gift to the spirits—tools to build a great canoe—they would be destroyed by another flood. First Man then went from lodge to lodge and collected the tools, which were first deposited in the medicine lodge and later cast into the river as an offering.

As depicted in this painting by Catlin, Mandan men join in a spirited contest to see who can shoot the most arrows into the air from the same bow before the first one released comes to earth. Each participant had to wager a valued possession, such as a bow, and the winner claimed all the prizes.

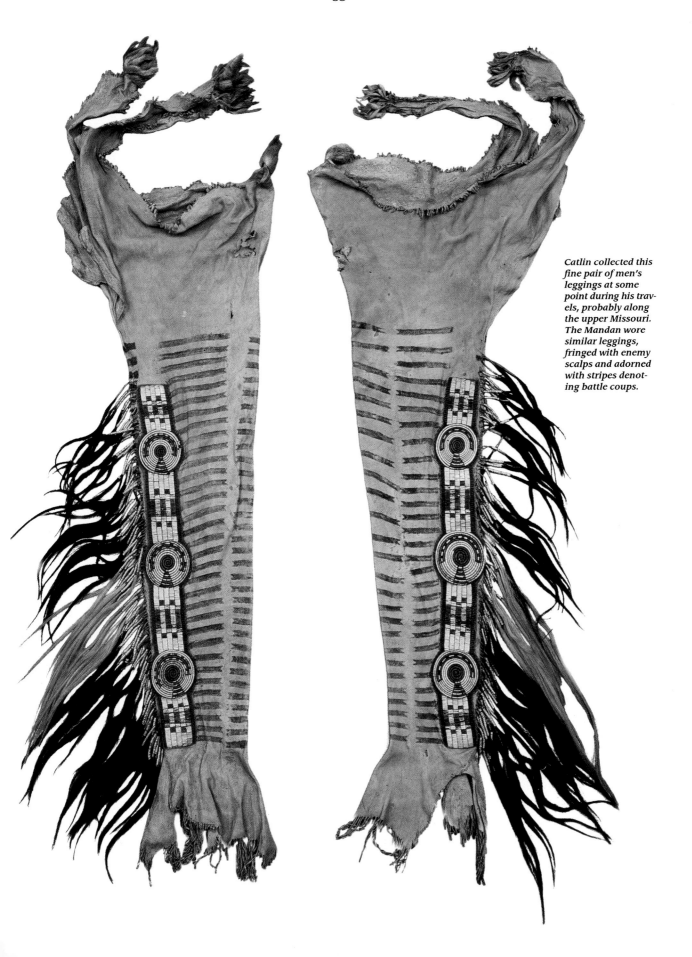

Catlin collected this fine pair of men's leggings at some point during his travels, probably along the upper Missouri. The Mandan wore similar leggings, fringed with enemy scalps and adorned with stripes denoting battle coups.

The following day, Catlin related, First Man conducted 50 devout young men into the medicine lodge. There they would go without food, water, and sleep for four days before enduring agony—including the insertion of barbs through their flesh—as proof of their devotion to the Great Spirit. Having committed the young men to their ordeal, First Man left the ritual in the hands of the keeper of the lodge and departed, explaining to the people that "he was going back to the mountains in the west" and promising to return in a year's time.

In documenting this remarkable ceremony, which included rousing dances by men wearing buffalo regalia and concluded with harrowing scenes of suffering, Catlin feared that the public would find his account incredible. He had agent Kipp and two aides sign a statement that his pictures and notes "faithfully represented those scenes as we saw them transacted, without any addition or exaggeration."

After spending the summer among the Mandan and Hidatsa, Catlin continued downriver to Saint Louis. His visit had been amicable and enlightening, but his departure was shadowed by an ominous incident. As he left Fort Clark in his canoe, a party of Mandans ran after him along the riverbank and gestured for him to come ashore. He did as they asked and learned that a girl he had recently portrayed had fallen gravely ill and was bleeding from the mouth. "The picture which you made of her is too much like her," one Mandan asserted. "You are drawing the strings out of her

This detailed interior view of a Mandan earth lodge was painted by Karl Bodmer during his visit as artist for the Maximilian expedition in the winter of 1833-1834. It shows the stout posts and crossbeams supporting the roof, and various implements and containers crafted by the villagers, including a burden basket like the one shown at right, used to carry crops. The lodge housed several related families.

heart and they will soon break. We must take her picture back and then she will get well again." With some reluctance, Catlin surrendered the portrait. "I have since learned that the girl died," he wrote later, "and that I am forever to be considered the cause of her misfortunes."

The following year, in November 1833, another expedition arrived to spend the winter at Fort Clark. This party was led by Prince Maximilian zu Wied, a German aristocrat who drew on his personal fortune to survey the tribal peoples of the upper Missouri River and their environment. Accompanying Maximilian was Swiss artist Karl Bodmer, who saw relatively little of Indian country compared with the wide-ranging Catlin but produced a series of watercolors among the Mandan and Hidatsa that rivaled Catlin's scenes for richness of detail. Bodmer not only portrayed the Mandan and Hidatsa with consummate skill but also studied their artistry and helped to encourage it.

On one occasion, Bodmer painted a Hidatsa chief, who was reluctant to leave the finished work in the artist's hands because he was going off to war and feared that some of his strength would remain behind in the portrait. In the end, the chief came up with a compromise. He drew a fine likeness of Bodmer, thus evening the score. Such attitudes were not so mysterious to Bodmer. He too believed in the power of images to capture the

An exterior sketch of a Mandan earth lodge by Bodmer reveals its sturdy roof, lined with willow rods and covered with insulating sod at all points except the entryway and central smoke hole.

spirit of people and places, and he recognized that Indian artistry owed much to their conviction that pictures were a potent form of medicine. Like Catlin, he was greatly impressed by Chief Mahtotohpa, who was both an accomplished warrior and a gifted artist, having recorded his exploits on buffalo robes. In homage to Mahtotohpa, Bodmer faithfully depicted one of those robes, showing the chief counting coup on his enemies. Supplied with materials by Bodmer, the chief then portrayed further scenes from his eventful life with pencil and watercolors. Mahtotohpa's efforts, like that of another Mandan warrior-artist, Sihchida (Yellow Feather), demonstrated that both men learned lessons from Bodmer during his stay, even as he drew inspiration from their work.

Sadly, the visit of Maximilian and Bodmer was among the last such revealing exchanges between the villagers and the outside world. In 1837 a trading vessel steaming upriver brought another deadly smallpox epidemic to the area. Only 100 or so members of the two tribes survived, and they abandoned their villages. Catlin learned later from agent Kipp that Mahtotohpa was among the survivors but saw his entire family perish and lost the will to live. Alone in his lodge, Mahtotohpa covered his dead kin with buffalo robes, Catlin related, "and wrapping another around himself, went out upon a hill at a little distance . . . resolved to starve himself to death. He remained there until the sixth day, when he had just strength enough to creep back to the village." Reentering his lodge, he lay down beside his loved ones, "drew his robe over him, and died on the ninth day."

Catlin concluded that the tribe had been extinguished: "So have perished the friendly and hospitable Mandans." Yet like their culture hero First

Man, those who survived the catastrophe rebuilt their shattered society. In the decades to come, the remaining Mandan and Hidatsa came to terms with the Arikara and formed the Three Affiliated Tribes on the Fort Berthold Reservation in North Dakota. Thus the villagers of the upper Missouri endured as a people. And a record of their ancestral culture survived as well in words and pictures, thanks to the keen observers who passed their way and the gracious tribal chroniclers who informed and enlightened them.

Catlin was not alone in prematurely consigning an afflicted tribe to extinction. Many people sympathetic to Indians feared at the time that they were a "vanishing race," a misconception that only made it easier for authorities to deny tribes a secure place in the nation's future. Few outsiders appreciated just how resilient Native Americans could be. But the sense of impending doom brought at least one blessing. It lent urgency to the study of native cultures, which were indeed undergoing dire changes. Ethnographers who set out to document "vanishing" traditions some-

Sihchida (Yellow Feather) of the Mandan is portrayed at left by Bodmer in a buffalo robe and feathered headdress, with otter fur around his neck and heel trailers proclaiming his exploits. Sihchida displayed his own artistry by using Bodmer's supplies to paint the watercolor below, possibly a self-portrait.

times became advocates for tribes that were fighting to preserve what remained of their land and their way of life.

One such supportive scholar was Lewis Henry Morgan, who grew up in the Finger Lakes district of New York in the early 1800s, just a few decades after whites ousted the Iroquois from that bountiful area. Like Catlin, Morgan was fascinated by Indians before he knew much about them. As a young lawyer in Rochester in the early 1840s, he organized a branch of a secret society known as the Order of the Gordian Knot and soon transformed it into something closer to his heart—the Grand Order of the Iroquois. His own chapter was dedicated to the Cayuga Nation, while others that formed in nearby cities were named after the Mohawk, the Oneida, the Onondaga, and the Seneca. At first, by Morgan's own admission, the activities of the Grand Order were little more than "boyish" diversions. Members wore Iroquois leggings and headdresses at their gettogethers, brandished tomahawks, and spoke in a stilted fashion that represented their dim notion of Indian oratory. As one member declared to another with mock solemnity: "The tall pine in the young forest has not spoken with a forked tongue."

Remarkably, Morgan managed to inject a serious purpose into this frivolous order. As he put it, he wanted the fraternity to become a "repository of all that remains to us of the Indian . . . his antiquities, customs, eloquence, history, and institutions." Under Morgan's guidance, members of the order began to read and discuss the few books available on the Iroquois. It was while rummaging through a bookstore in Albany in 1844 that Morgan met the individual who shaped his career as an ethnographer—a young Seneca named Hasanoanda, or Ely Samuel Parker. Raised on the Tonawanda Reservation near Buffalo, Parker had been educated at a school run by a Baptist missionary. Such was his proficiency in English that at age 16 he was already serving as an interpreter for a Seneca delegation to the state capital. Parker invited Morgan to meet the delegates, and Morgan plied them with questions about their traditions for "as long as propriety would permit," recording their answers in his notebook as Parker translated.

The meeting of Parker and Morgan proved rewarding for both sides. Morgan's Grand Order elected Parker an honorary member, invited him to speak on the travails of his people during the reservation era, and financed his further education at a nearby academy. The Seneca wanted Parker to study law so that he could help them in their efforts to resist removal from their Tonawanda Reservation to an uncertain destination west of the Mississippi River. Parker read law diligently but was denied

Seneca spokesman Ely Samuel Parker, shown here in 1855, worked closely with ethnographer Lewis Henry Morgan to produce the landmark study "League of the Ho-de-no-sau-nee, or Iroquois," one of the first accounts to evaluate an American Indian culture by its own standards.

admission to the bar because, as an Indian, he had not been granted citizenship. Instead, he became a civil engineer. During the Civil War, he served in the Union Army as an engineer and rose to become a trusted aide of General Ulysses S. Grant, who later as president named Parker commissioner of Indian affairs—the first Native American to serve in that position.

While Morgan played a small part in furthering this remarkable career, young Parker rendered crucial assistance to the aspiring ethnographer. Morgan's interview with the Seneca delegation in Albany was just the first of many contacts with the Iroquois that Parker arranged for him and contributed to as interpreter. By 1846 Morgan had so gained the trust of the Iroquois that he and two white assistants were formally adopted by the Seneca at Tonawanda. Ely Parker attended the ceremony, marked by war dances, and wrote with mixed feelings about a people who had once dominated the country and intimidated colonists celebrating the induction of "white brothers into their nation."

As an adopted member of the Hawk Clan, Morgan now had access to rituals and lore that had previously been closed to him. With Parker's help, Morgan filled scores of notebooks with data that formed the basis for a landmark study of the Iroquois, published in 1851—a book later praised by explorer and ethnographer John Wesley Powell as the "first scientific account of an Indian tribe given to the world."

Morgan announced his intention to portray Iroquois culture on its own terms in the title of the book: *League of the Ho-de-no-sau-nee, or Iroquois.* As Morgan explained, the Iroquois called themselves the Hodenosaunee, or People of the Longhouse, to express the deep sense of kinship that bound together their tribes, or nations, as one body. "They likened their confederacy to a longhouse," he wrote, "having partitions and separate fires, after their ancient method of building houses, within which the several nations were sheltered under a common roof." The Mohawk guarded the eastern door to this longhouse, and the Seneca guarded the western door, with the other nations dwelling in between, each with its own fire. By adopting the imagery of the Iroquois, Morgan shared with readers the insights he had gained when Parker and others welcomed him under their roof.

Morgan described in detail not only the political rituals that unified the confederacy but also the cycle of religious ceremonies that bound Iroquois communities together through the year. Morgan treated those observances with great respect, even when discussing rituals such as the Sacrifice of the White Dog that seemed alien to the Christian tradition he was raised in and still adhered to. On the first day of their midwinter rite, Morgan reported, Iroquois ceremonial leaders "selected a dog, free from physical blemish, and of a pure white," and strangled the animal, taking care not to shed its blood or break any bones. Far from feeling contempt for the victim, worshipers regarded the animal as blessed. "White was the Iroquois emblem of purity and of faith," Morgan noted, and the fidelity of the dog to its keeper was emblematic of their devotion to the supreme power. No more trustworthy messenger "could be found to bear their petitions to the Master of life." Later, worshipers burned the body of the dog on a wooden altar as a priest offered a prayer to the Great Spirit: "We now obey thy commands. That which thou hast made is returning unto thee. It is rising to thee, by which it will appear that our words are true."

This and other speeches that Parker translated and Morgan wove into the text were a far cry from the fanciful Indian oratory found in fiction and mimicked by members of the Grand Order before they knew better. Parker and Morgan conveyed the

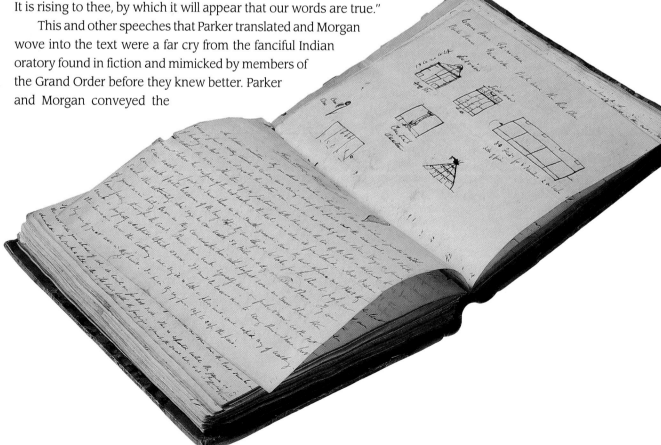

power of Iroquois rhetoric in words that rang clear and true, as in this prayer of thanksgiving: "We return thanks to our mother, the earth, which sustains us. We return thanks to the rivers and streams, which supply us with water. We return thanks to all herbs, which furnish medicines for the cure of diseases. We return thanks to the corn, and to her sisters, the beans and squashes, which give us life. We return thanks to the bushes and trees, which provide us with fruit. We return thanks to the wind, which, moving the air, has banished diseases. We return thanks to the moon and stars, which have given to us their light when the sun was gone."

Morgan acknowledged his debt to Parker by dedicating the book to him and describing it as the "fruit of our joint researches." In his preface, Morgan expressed the hope that the book would "encourage a kinder feeling toward the Indian, founded upon a truer knowledge of his civil and domestic institutions." The truths Morgan arrived at came not from detached observation but from a relationship between the author and the Iroquois that went beyond the confines of research. As part of that relationship, Morgan lent support to Tonawanda Senecas in their campaign to overturn an 1840 treaty that required them to abandon their reservation and emigrate to the west. The treaty makers, by offering inducements that in some cases amounted to bribes, had obtained the signatures of a bare majority of the 90 or so chiefs on the reservation council. Senecas fought the treaty on several grounds, including one that went to the heart of their culture—the need for the unanimous consent of council members. Traditionally, if such unanimity was not achieved, the chiefs ended deliberations and doused the council fire, postponing action until they could reach a consensus, or "roll their words into one bundle." Senecas refused to recognize as binding a treaty signed under duress by a mere majority.

Members of Morgan's Grand Order circulated petitions on behalf of the Senecas, and he himself delivered the statements of support to Washington. Another ethnographer, Henry Rowe Schoolcraft, who had served as federal Indian agent in the Great Lakes region and negotiated several treaties there, testified before the Senate

Lewis Henry Morgan made the notes and sketches at left during a field trip to the Tonawanda Reservation in western New York in 1849. Sketched on the right-hand page of the notebook are views of a traditional Iroquois lodge like the one portrayed in the lithograph below, made of a framework of poles covered with slabs of bark.

GÄ-NÓ-SOTE
or
BARK HOUSE.

DÄ-AH-DE-A

A SENECA IN THE COSTUME OF THE IROQUOIS.

As part of his fieldwork, Morgan collected and sketched traditional Iroquois apparel such as the items worn at left by Levi Parker, Ely Parker's brother, and portrayed in detail at right. Morgan described the headdress—a silk cap topped with an eagle feather—as the "most conspicuous part of the male costume." The kilt, he noted, resembled that of Scottish Highlanders, while the moccasin was among the finest articles "for the protection and adornment of the foot ever invented."

CUS-TO-WEH or HEAD DRESS.

GÄ-KÄ-AH or KILT.

that the Tonawanda agreement indeed violated the Iroquois principle of unanimous consent. Ely Parker argued eloquently for his people before the same committee, but in the end, the senators let the treaty stand, claiming that to do otherwise would "open a field of interminable difficulties, embarrassment, and expense." Senecas kept up the fight, however, and in 1857, they won the right to repurchase part of the Tonawanda Reservation with funds set aside for their removal to Kansas. The community that had nurtured the pioneering work of Parker and Morgan would continue to exist.

In the decades to come, other ethnographers would go beyond fieldwork and try to help the Indians by becoming involved in tribal affairs. But such involvement carried risks. There were deep divisions on reservations between people who favored the old ways and those pursuing new paths; outsiders who aided one camp often incurred the hostility of the other. Furthermore, plans to improve the lot of reservation dwellers sometimes did more harm than good. The conflict between the urge to study tribal culture and the desire to reform it was exemplified by the career of Alice Cunningham Fletcher, who worked among Indians both as an ethnographer and as an administrator of a far-reaching federal program aimed at assimilating tribespeople into the larger society.

Fletcher appeared to be an unlikely candidate for either task. Raised in a fashionable section of Brooklyn in a household dominated by her stern stepfather, who allowed her to read no fiction other than the novels of Charles Dickens, she attended private academies and worked as a governess and teacher before making her mark as a lecturer on a variety of topics, including temperance, feminism, and the monuments of the mound builders and other ancient Americans. Not until she was in her forties did she become interested in contemporary Indians. In 1880 she met on the lecture circuit the young Omaha spokeswoman, Susette La Flesche, and her half-brother, Francis, who were touring the East with the Ponca chief, Standing Bear, to elicit public support for the Ponca in their campaign to resist removal from their Nebraska homeland. As Fletcher learned, the Omaha were close to the Ponca culturally and geographically and were involved in their own land dispute with the federal government.

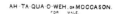

AH-TA-QUA-O-WEH, or MOCCASON.
FOR MALE.

Unencumbered by family ties and hungry for enlightenment and adventure, she resolved to visit their country and study firsthand the culture and conditions of the region's tribes.

Her first field trip began inauspiciously. In September 1881, she headed west to Nebraska and embarked with a small party that included Susette and her white husband, newspaperman Thomas Henry Tibbles, on an arduous wagon journey through Omaha and Ponca territory to the Rosebud Reservation of the Lakota Sioux in South Dakota. As Tibbles noted, the trip was marred by thunderstorms, muddy roads, a balky pony, and winds that blistered Fletcher's face, "but that city-bred lady stood everything without one complaint." More disconcerting to Fletcher than the physical hardship was the shock of confronting a culture so unlike her own among the Lakota, who had abandoned violent resistance to federal authorities just a few years earlier. "I felt a foreignness that grew into a sense of isolation," she wrote of a Lakota dance she attended. "I was oppressed with its strangeness." At first, she confessed, the dance called to her mind tales of "Indian atrocities." Yet when Tibbles suggested that they leave early, she insisted on staying to learn more about the ceremony.

In time she proved so insistent in querying holy men as to the meaning of their rituals that some Lakotas regarded it as sacrilege and warned that misfortune would befall the tribe as a result. One priest asked her to promise him by her God "that no harm shall come to me or to my people because I have spoken to you of these sacred things." Fletcher replied that only God could offer such an assurance, but promised to pray that no evil came to the Lakota. The priest accepted her pledge, and she was able to continue her studies, which bore fruit in a series of articles that described such hitherto-secret rituals as the Lakota White Buffalo Ceremony and offered valuable insights into the nature of Indian spirituality. She refuted the common notion that Indians worshiped animals or objects in nature such as the moon or the sun, pointing out that the spirits they prayed to were transcendent beings that visited worldly objects and infused them with power. When Indians praised the buffalo or the radiant disk of the sun, she wrote, they were honoring places "where the god has stopped."

Fletcher did her most important ethnographic work among the Omaha, in collaboration with Francis La Flesche. Like other members of his gifted family, Francis was educated by whites at the insistence of his father, Joseph La Flesche, a tribal chief of mixed Omaha, Ponca, and French ancestry. Although well assimilated, Francis was proud of his Omaha heritage and intent on preserving a record of tribal traditions that were eroding un-

Francis La Flesche of the Omaha tribe sits at left beside his sister Susette in 1879 during a lecture tour of the East on behalf of Indian reform. Later on the tour, he met Alice Fletcher and helped inspire her to take to the field as an ethnographer. Working together, he and Fletcher produced a definitive study of traditional Omaha culture.

der pressure from outside forces. In Alice Fletcher, he found a colleague with the talent and influence to bring their joint efforts before the public. Nearly 20 years younger than she was, he looked to her for personal support as well as for professional guidance. In time, he was informally adopted by Fletcher. The relationship struck some whites who knew them as odd, but it had strong precedents in Indian culture. When the Ojibwa named Wawatam adopted trader Alexander Henry, for example, he embraced him as a "son, brother, and friend." In much the same way, Fletcher served La Flesche as a mother, a sister, and a partner in research. Their collaboration culminated in a joint study, *The Omaha Tribe,* which ranked with Morgan and Parker's work on the Iroquois as a classic of ethnography.

Fletcher's association with Francis La Flesche and his family aided her immeasurably as a scholar, but through them she also became embroiled in reservation politics. When she first visited the Omaha Reservation in 1881, Joseph La Flesche and his kin were living there with like-minded members of the tribe in a cluster of frame houses that some Omahas derided as the "village of the make-believe white men." Joseph La Flesche wanted the federal government to enact an 1854 treaty that had since stalled in Congress. It called for part of the reservation to be surveyed into parcels that would be allotted to those who volunteered. A number of Omahas opposed this plan, believing that all land should be held in common by the tribe. But Fletcher sympathized with La Flesche and his supporters. Here as elsewhere, surrounding whites were eager to remove the Indians, and Fletcher feared that Omahas might lose all if they did not obtain legal title to individual allotments.

Returning east, she drew up an amended allotment bill for the Omaha and guided it through Congress, often gaining access to representatives through their wives and daughters, who attended her lectures and offered her support. Unlike the original treaty, Fletcher's bill specified that allotment would apply to all Omahas. Any land remaining after tribal members received their 160-acre parcels would be sold to white settlers. The bill served as a precedent for the General Allotment Act, sponsored by Senator Henry L. Dawes, which called for the allotment of reservations across the country.

At the time, allotment was supported by many whites who were sympathetic to Indians but failed to grasp how trying it would be for reservation dwellers to renounce their collective identity and merge with an American society that had been largely hostile to them in the past. In backing allotment, Fletcher reflected the views of other ethnographers, including Lewis Henry Morgan. After working with the Iroquois, Morgan had embarked on a comparative study of tribal cultures that led him to argue that American Indians occupied an intermediate stage in the scale of social evolution between "savagery" and "civilization." Although Morgan and Fletcher saw much to be admired in tribal cultures, they agreed with most legislators and scholars in the field that Indians should be encouraged to abandon tribalism and progress down the path toward "civilization" through ownership of private property and other forms of assimilation.

So strong was Fletcher's commitment to the idea that she agreed to administer the allotment process, first for the Omaha and later for the Winnebago and Nez Perce. Returning to the Omaha Reservation in 1883, she met with stout resistance from a group known as the Council Fire, who opposed both allotment and the education of their children by whites. When Fletcher was left bedridden by an injury to her knee, complicated by arthritis, her opponents took heart. The Council Fire "glowed brightly," she wrote, and their "numbers and influence increased, and showed itself in a widespread refusal to send the children to school; and a general outcry that the old religion would revive and the old times return, for was not the woman who had been so strong struck down and kept there by a spell thrown upon her by the ancient charms?"

Although her knee remained permanently impaired, she recovered her strength, helped on by Francis La Flesche and kin, who sang songs of healing for her. By late fall, she had allotted two-thirds of the reservation to volunteers. Faced with unflinching opposition from the Council Fire, she laid

Alice Fletcher, appointed to administer the federal allotment of the Nez Perce Reservation in Idaho in 1889, meets there with Chief Joseph (center) accompanied by her interpreter, James Stuart, shown kneeling in this photograph taken by Fletcher's aide, E. Jane Gay. During her assignment, Fletcher collected examples of tribal handiwork, including the finely woven bag at left, which was given to her by James Stuart and used traditionally for root gathering and storage.

down the law. Reservation police summoned the resisters to her office. One by one, they made their marks on the allotment papers she laid before them, knowing that if they did not the local Indian agent could confine them to the reservation and otherwise restrict their activities.

When Fletcher set out in 1889 to allot the Nez Perce Reservation in Idaho, she faced even broader resistance. As she admitted in a letter to an acquaintance, the reservation land was not well suited for farming, and the allotments offered to the Nez Perce were probably too small to allow for profitable grazing. She never voiced such doubts in public, but another member of her party offered vivid testimony as to the pitfalls of the allotment plan. E. Jane Gay, a close friend and associate of Fletcher's, accompanied her to Idaho as housekeeper and chronicled the experience in photographs and in a revealing series of letters published in a journal back east.

In principle, Gay supported Fletcher in her assignment, but she was sensitive to the qualms of the reservation dwellers, who had heard nothing of the allotment program before Fletcher and her party arrived. The Nez Perce had not forgotten the relentless campaign by the U.S. Army in 1877 to force the defiant Chief Joseph and his followers onto the reservation. Joseph and other Nez Perce fugitives taken captive in Montana that fall had spent eight years in bitter exile in the Indian Territory before being allowed to return to the Northwest. Chief Joseph consented to meet with Fletcher and told her he would accept an allotment—but only in the Wallowa Valley,

Among the items collected by Fletcher from the Nez Perce was this club, topped with a stone and covered with rawhide. Despite her busy schedule in Idaho, Fletcher found time to take field notes on tribal traditions and to acquire this and other artifacts for the Peabody Museum at Harvard University.

his beloved homeland in Oregon that he had been forced by troops to relinquish to white settlers. Fletcher had no authority to grant his request, and Joseph told her he would rather remain "landless and homeless" than settle for anything less. "It was good to see an unsubjugated Indian," Gay wrote after the meeting. "One could not help respecting the man who still stood firmly for his rights."

When Fletcher first stood before a crowd of Nez Perces at the Lapwai Agency to explain the allotment program, Gay noted, she did so with "reddened cheeks and stammering tongue." Even the normally confident Fletcher, referred to by Gay as "Her Majesty," found it difficult to explain how dividing the reservation into small parts and selling off the rest would bring the Nez Perce something greater than the whole that they now possessed. Granted, ranchers and other intruders were nibbling at the margins of the reservation, but what was to keep them from devouring Indian land even after allotment? As Gay noted, Fletcher knew better than to say to the long-suffering Nez Perce: "'I am your friend.' That phrase means nothing now to the Indian."

After meeting with skepticism in Lapwai, Fletcher moved on to the Christian mission community of Kamiah in the hope of a better reception. Even there, however, people were reluctant to have their homeland "cut up in little pieces," as one man put it. Fletcher was heartened when the Nez Perce pastor there, Robert Williams, volunteered to become the first in the area to register for an allotment. After him, Gay noted, some of his friends and kin "dropped in, one by one, at first as if it were a serious surgical operation to be registered; some as if ashamed to come and others as if afraid." Fletcher and Gay stood up for the minister by helping to refurbish his faded church, but their conspicuous support for Williams only widened the rift in the congregation between those in favor of allotment and those opposed.

Over the course of four summers, the persistent Fletcher, known to the Nez Perce as the Measuring Woman, rode back and forth across the rugged Idaho reservation despite her crippled leg and induced most members of the tribe to bow to the inevitable and accept the program. She registered nearly 2,000 allotments totaling 179,000 acres, leaving more than 500,000 acres to be sold to whites. Proceeds from the sale brought the Nez Perce a few years of prosperity, but later, many were unable to make a living on their allotments and had to lease their land to outsiders and move to the agency.

When Fletcher and company left the reservation in 1892, they had no way of knowing the ultimate effect of their actions on the Nez Perce. But they had seen ample evidence of how disturbing their involvement in tribal affairs could be to reservation dwellers. The summer before, Jane Gay had been approached by Nez Perce Christians who complained that the forthcoming Fourth of July celebration at Lapwai contained war processions, lewd behavior, gambling, and other practices that violated their own religious principles and the values authorities were trying to instill in the tribe as a whole. Gay encouraged them to write to the commissioner of Indian affairs, and an edict came down forbidding the war procession and horse racing and gambling on the school grounds. Many Nez Perces were incensed because the Fourth of July was their own Independence Day, honoring both an ancestral midsummer festival of the tribe and the return of followers of Chief Joseph to the reservation on July 4, 1885. In the end, there was no war procession, but people raced and gambled freely near the school grounds. "For a whole week," Gay wrote, "the ponies galloped and the blankets were staked and lost and won." Unnerved by the hostile reaction to the letter, she slept with a pistol under her pillow.

Alice Fletcher, standing at far left, called this meeting to explain the allotment process to Nez Perces at the First Presbyterian Church in Kamiah, near the eastern edge of the reservation. Despite heated opposition to the allotment program, Fletcher vowed in a letter to a friend to see the task through: "I will get the work done and before long, I trust."

BUREAU OF ETHNOLOGY.

EIGHTH ANNUAL REPORT PL. CXX.

E.

N.

S.

W.

FIRST SAND PAINTING.

RESEARCHING TRIBAL LORE

As more and more researchers took to the field in the 19th century to document Indian lifeways, a new discipline emerged—ethnology, or the comparative study of tribal cultures. In 1879 that discipline won formal recognition when the Smithsonian Institution established the Bureau of Ethnology to promote systematic fieldwork and compile reports from around the continent.

The driving force behind the bureau was its director for the first 23 years, John Wesley Powell, an avid explorer and geologist as well as a pioneering ethnologist. Powell was largely self-taught, and he supported other independent scholars with little academic training, such as Frank Hamilton Cushing, who joined in an important Smithsonian expedition to the Southwest in 1879. But Powell also helped systematize ethnographic research by insisting that fieldworkers take careful notes and submit thorough reports, which together offered a broad view of American Indian culture. As shown here, the bureau's comprehensive annual reports often featured illustrations drawn by Indians themselves or inspired by their artistry.

Illustrations for an article on a nine-day Navajo healing ceremony, published in the Bureau of Ethnology's Eighth Annual Report, show a patient kneeling by a sweat house (right), which he must enter feetfirst; and a sand painting (above), designed to lure sacred beings down to earth so they can remove the patient's illness.

47TH CONGRESS, } HOUSE OF REPRESENTATIVES. { MIS. DOC.
1st Session. { } No. 61.

SECOND ANNUAL REPORT

OF THE

BUREAU OF ETHNOLOGY

TO THE

SECRETARY OF THE SMITHSONIAN INSTITUTION

1880-'81

BY

J. W. POWELL
DIRECTOR

WASHINGTON
GOVERNMENT PRINTING OFFICE
1883

The frontispiece of the Second Annual Report bears the bureau's insignia, an Indian cliff dwelling beneath a storm-cloud motif of the sort found in native southwestern painting. This issue included articles on Zuni fetishes, Iroquois legends, and the culture of the ancient Mississippian mound builders.

John Wesley Powell, pictured here behind his desk at the bureau he headed, made a forbidding impression with his rugged beard and piercing eyes. But he was well liked by his staff and promoted the careers of promising young scholars.

The bureau's annual report for 1899-1900 featured these Hopi drawings of kachinas—spirits residing in the mountains, who were said to return to the pueblo each winter to help renew the world's bounty and sustain the people. As portrayed here, Hopi men impersonated kachinas during ceremonies by wearing elaborate wooden masks and dancing to invoke the blessings of the spirits.

After completing the fractious Nez Perce allotment, Fletcher returned with some relief to ethnography. As she now realized, however, even scholarly intrusions could provoke strong tribal opposition. In recent years, she and Francis La Flesche had been acquiring ritual objects of the Omaha for preservation in museums lest they decay or fall into the hands of unscrupulous collectors. The fact that curators intended to preserve the objects for display hardly consoled Omahas who honored the old ways, however. They were deeply troubled when La Flesche asked a priest named Shudenaci (Yellow Smoke) to part with the Sacred Pole, also known as the Venerable Man, long the centerpiece of a ritual that honored leading men of the tribe as hunters and warriors. The ritual was no longer performed, but Shudenaci feared that by surrendering the pole and revealing its mysteries he would fall under a curse. Only after old Joseph La Flesche pledged to take upon himself any curse associated with divulging the secrets did Shudenaci open up to the ethnographers. A few days later, Joseph La Flesche fell ill, and within two weeks he was dead. Some took it as proof of the Sacred Pole's enduring power. But Francis La Flesche was undeterred. Lamenting that some of his people still lived "in the shades of superstition," he carried on with his work.

About the time that Alice Fletcher first visited the Omaha and became caught up in the issues of reservation policy, a young man named Frank Hamilton Cushing was immersing himself in the time-honored traditions of an Indian tribe in a way no ethnographer had ever before attempted. Predecessors such as Catlin and Morgan had spent weeks or months with the Indians they were studying, but Cushing lived among the Zuni of New Mexico for more than four years. During that time, he was adopted by the tribe's governor, learned to speak as the Zuni did, and gained entry to their most prestigious secret society, the Priesthood of the Bow. In some ways, his experience resembled that of adopted captives like John Tanner and James Smith. But Cushing went deliberately among the Zuni, and he brought with him uncommon powers of observation and interpretation that allowed him to translate what he learned into a penetrating portrait of the culture.

Raised in western New York by a free-thinking physician who cared little for formal schooling and allowed him to spend much of his time roaming the forest, young Cushing collected arrowheads and other Indian artifacts and learned on his own how to reproduce them in native fashion by working flint with a bone tool. A paper he published at the age of 17 on the natural history of his home woods won him a job the following year at the Smithsonian Institution in Washington, D.C. In 1879, when Cushing was just 22, he was sent by the Smithsonian to the Southwest as part of a collecting expedition. Cushing's job was to gather Zuni artifacts and find out all he could about the people who produced them. It was no easy task. The Zuni, like other Pueblo peoples of the Southwest, had managed through secrecy and occasional acts of defiance to preserve their rich ceremonial traditions despite a long history of outside interference, first by Spanish colonizers and more recently by Anglo-Americans. Many tribal groups around the country were reluctant to open their hearts and their sanctuaries to outsiders. But Pueblo peoples were especially wary of meddlesome strangers, having spent centuries deflecting the unwelcome advances of conquistadors, friars, treasure hunters, and Indian agents.

The flamboyant Frank Hamilton Cushing, costumed here in Navajo dress with added Spanish touches, came to the Southwest on the 1879 Smithsonian expedition but parted company with the other researchers and remained at Zuni Pueblo (right), where he lived for several years as part of the community. Although Cushing followed his own path, he retained the respect of John Wesley Powell, who called him a "man of genius."

At first, Cushing behaved in a way that seemed to confirm the fears of his hosts. Young and brash, he strode about the pueblo, making notes and sketching the people and their ceremonies without asking permission. On one occasion, he portrayed a sacred dance, to the vocal dismay of the onlookers. "When I took my station on a housetop, sketchbooks and colors in hand," he recalled, "I was surprised to see frowns and hear explosive, angry expostulations in every direction." One old woman grabbed his book "and pantomimically tore it to pieces. I was chagrined, but paid no attention to her, forced a good-natured smile, and continued my sketching. Discouraged, yet far from satisfied, the natives made no further demonstration."

Cushing concluded that he would never overcome the resistance of the Zuni so long as he lived apart from them, outside the pueblo with other members of the expedition. So he packed up his belongings and moved uninvited into the home of the Zuni governor, Palowahtiwa. There, "on the dirt floor in one corner," Cushing wrote, he spread his blankets and slung a hammock from the rafters. When the governor came home that evening to find the young man ensconced, he asked him pointedly: "How long will it be before you go back to Washington?" Informed that he could expect Cushing's company for at least two months, he uttered an oath and and left his "guest" to his own devices.

Palowahtiwa was in no position to defy the authorities in Washington who sent Cushing to the pueblo. Furthermore, he recognized that the young man, for all his presumption, was sincerely interested in the Zuni and open to instruction. Cushing's training began that very night, when he attempted to fry up some old bacon for supper. As he related, the fumes soon drew the attention of the governor, who "regarded bacon as vile" and would not have it consumed under his roof. Seizing the skillet, Palowahtiwa "marched down to the river. When he returned, every trace of the odious bacon had been removed, and replaced by a liberal quantity of mutton and abundant suet. Poking up the fire, the old fellow dexterously cooked the contents brown." After consuming the meal and falling asleep, Cushing awoke the next morning to find the governor "busily engaged in preparing a breakfast for me." Palowahtiwa performed such courtesies not as Cushing's servant but as his patron and guardian, whose task it was to educate this promising but uncouth young man in the ways of the Zuni.

After two months, the Smithsonian expedition moved on to continue their collecting among the nearby Hopi, but Cushing chose to remain with the governor and his people. He fully expected to be allotted provisions by the expedition leaders, but they left him empty-handed. Alone and utterly dependent on the Zuni, he could not disguise his despair from Palowahtiwa. "Little Brother," the governor counseled him, "you may be a Washington man, but it seems you are very poor. Now, if you do as we tell you, and will only make up your mind to be a Zuni, you shall be rich, for you shall have fathers and mothers, brothers and sisters, and the best food in the world."

Palowahtiwa hoped that as Cushing became one with the Zuni, he would leave his "books and pencils behind" and join in their ceremonies as a participant rather than as an observer. But Cushing was intent on playing both parts. Indeed, he was credited by later ethnographers with inventing the dual role of participant-observer. On one occasion, when he persisted in sketching a holy dance of the Zuni from a rooftop, two sacred clowns—who regaled the onlookers during the interludes on such occasions—

Zunis who accompanied Cushing on a trip east in 1882 pose in their native dress in Boston. Cushing and his guests were members of the Priesthood of the Bow, a Zuni warrior society whose sacred shield—shown at right above a mountain lion fetish belonging to the priesthood—bore the imposing image of a war god called the Knife-feathered Monster, with wings spread.

BUREAU OF ETHNOLOGY.   SECOND ANNUAL REPORT 1881 PL. X.

1

2

SHIELD AND FETICH OF THE PRIESTHOOD OF THE BOW.

threatened him with war clubs. Cushing managed a smile, waved his hunting knife so that it glinted in the sun, and proudly displayed his sketchbook, whereupon the clowns backed off and pronounced him a friend. Cushing regarded this show of force by the clowns as a serious act of intimidation, if not an outright threat to his life. But their role was to protect the pueblo symbolically, through taunts and gestures. Fortunately, Cushing responded to their feint with a pantomime of his own, and the onlookers gave him credit for playing along. "Never afterward," he wrote, "was I molested to any serious extent in attempting to make notes and sketches."

Gradually, Cushing was drawn deeper into the life of the tribe under the supervision of the governor, who dressed him as a Zuni and removed his hammock, insisting that he sleep on the ground. "If you get cold," he told Cushing, "take off all your clothes and sleep next to the sheepskins and *think* you are warm, as the Zuni does. You must sleep in the cold and on a hard bed; that will harden your meat." As Cushing discovered, the Zuni believed that all youngsters entered the world soft and pliable, like raw dough or an unfired pot, and had to be hardened to achieve maturity. The first night he slept as the Zuni did, he suffered much discomfort, but he assured the governor that he had passed a good night and accepted his "hard fate."

A short time later, he was formally adopted by Palowahtiwa in a ceremony that included the piercing of his ears and blessings in which he was honored as a Child of the Sun—the same tribute Indians had offered more than three centuries earlier to Cabeza de Vaca and his Spanish companions as they trekked across the Southwest. Like them, Cushing was seen as being endowed with medicine, or healing power. Indeed, the Zuni gave him the adoptive name of Tenatsali, or Medicine Flower, after a "magical plant which grew on a single mountain in the west, the flowers of which were the most beautiful in the world, and of many colors, and the roots and juices of which were a panacea for all injuries to the flesh of man."

Cushing sometimes acted as a healer among the Zuni by cleansing sores and performing other simple operations. But his great service to the tribe was to articulate in writing the wondrous intricacy of their customs and beliefs. He described, among other practices, the sacred observances of the many Zuni medicine orders, or secret societies, including the Priesthood of the Bow, into which he was initiated after two years at the pueblo. A warrior society whose members also played a leading role in the community in peacetime, the Bow Priests dedicated their rituals to the mythical twins—children of the God of the Sun—who according to legend, guided the original Zuni from their place of origin deep within the womb of the earth and taught them how to survive in the daylight world and prevail over their enemies.

Cushing related how the ancient Zuni, with the aid of the twins, found their home in the middle of the world, between the lower realm of their progenitors and the upper realm of the sun god, the supreme power. Their universe had six directions—lower and upper, north and south, east and west—and a midpoint, or navel, situated at the heart of the pueblo. Each direction had a special quality and color and was associated with certain clans. The south, for example, was linked with summertime, fertility, and fire; with the color red; and with the Corn, Tobacco, and Badger Clans. The corn crop itself was central to the life of the Zuni, Cushing observed, and embraced all the directions, colors, and qualities in their universe. As related in a Zuni story he transcribed, one strain of maize "is of the Northland, yellow like the light of winter; the second is of the West, blue like the great world of waters; the third is of the South, red like the land of Everlasting Summer; the fourth is of the East, white like the land whence the sun brings the daylight; the fifth is of the upper regions, many-colored as are the clouds of morning and evening; and the sixth is of the lower regions, black as are the caves whence came we."

German-born Franz Boas (top) moved to the United States in 1886 and became a leading figure in American anthropology with the help of George Hunt (above), a Kwakiutl who served as an interpreter and collector for Boas and contributed to his influential writings and exhibits on northwestern tribal culture.

Like other ethnographers, Cushing owed such poetic insights to his tribal informants, including the governor, who freely divulged Zuni legends and lore to his "younger brother" from Washington. Cushing reciprocated by relating European legends for the Zuni and by inviting Palowahtiwa and other Zunis to accompany him back east when he returned there briefly in 1882 and again a few years later. On the latter occasion, Palowahtiwa noted with dismay that Cushing abandoned the prayers and tributes to the gods he had offered regularly among the Zuni. "So far as I can see, you are an American, not a Zuni," the governor declared. He reminded Cushing that he had been adopted not just by the Zuni but by their gods: "You became their child, as we are their children. Are you not now as then, their relative?"

Cushing replied that he still honored the gods after his fashion, but the question haunted him. Before he died in 1900, at age 43, his keen professional curiosity brought him in touch with many other peoples, yet none claimed him as the Zuni had. In 1938, 50 years after Cushing last visited the pueblo, archaeologist Bertha Dutton met elders there who still remembered Medicine Flower and mourned for him as for a long-lost kinsman.

Frank Cushing's fruitful relationship with Palowahtiwa, like that of Lewis Henry Morgan with Ely Parker and Alice Fletcher with Francis La Flesche, demonstrated the vital role played by Indians in shaping the ethnographic record of their people. Few tribal members did more in this way to promote understanding of their culture than George Hunt of British Columbia's Kwakiutl. Like La Flesche, Hunt was of mixed ancestry. His father was an English trader for the Hudson's Bay Company who married a woman of Alaska's Tlingit tribe and settled with her at Fort Rupert, a

A Kwakiutl chief in a button blanket arrives at a potlatch given by Franz Boas on November 28, 1894, in Fort Rupert, British Columbia. George Hunt instructed Boas in the art of staging a potlatch and bestowing gifts on the assembled guests, who then felt obliged to Boas. Kwakiutls called him the "silent one," because he did not know their language and asked Hunt to speak for him.

Kwakiutl community at the northern end of Vancouver Island. Born there in 1854, George Hunt was raised among Kwakiutls who traded actively with whites but retained many of their ancestral traditions, including competitive displays of wealth and status known as potlatches, and elaborate winter ceremonies, during which secret societies initiated new members amid great pageantry.

As a youngster of foreign ancestry, Hunt did not inherit the right to join a secret society or to stage a potlatch. But he married into the Kwakiutl and so gained entry to their ceremonial life. Through his wife's brother, he acquired membership in the prestigious Hamatsa Society, whose initiates attributed their sacred powers to a fearsome cannibal spirit. Thus Hunt, who could speak English as well as the local Kwakiutl dialect, was ideally placed to serve as a mediator between the tribe and outsiders eager to document their culture. Among those with whom he collaborated were

This diorama showing Kwakiutls preparing and weaving strands of cedar bark was among many displays Franz Boas prepared in the early 1900s as curator at the American Museum of Natural History. George Hunt collected some 2,500 tribal artifacts for Boas and the museum—including the ingenious Kwakiutl mask at right, depicting two guises of the legendary figure Raven, whose beak opens wide to reveal the face within.

photographer Edward Curtis and anthropologist Franz Boas, whose work with Hunt did much to dispel the tired notion that tribal peoples were worth studying only as examples of the so-called primitive state that civilized societies had emerged from.

The German-born Boas first visited the Kwakiutl in 1887, at the age of 29, a few years after completing his first field trip, to Baffin Island, north of Hudson Bay. There he had passed a hard winter among the local Inuit, surveying their terrain and studying their lore. As he traveled with the people by dogsled, slept alongside them in their igloos, and feasted with them on raw seal meat, the diffident young scholar lost his detachment. The Inuit called him Doctora'dluk, or Big Doctor, and he obliged them by dispensing food or simple medicines to victims of diphtheria and other European-borne diseases. Amid such perils, the Inuit made a profound impression on Boas by sharing their blessings with one another as freely as they did their sorrows. He praised them in a letter to his fiancée, using words of lasting import for the discipline of anthropology that Boas helped to establish: "Is it not a beautiful custom among these 'savages' that they bear all deprivation in common, and also are at their happiest best—eating and drinking—when someone has brought back booty from the hunt? I often ask myself what advantages our 'good society' possesses over that of the 'savages' and find, the more I see of their customs, that we have no right to look down upon them."

Among the Kwakiutl, Boas found further evidence to support his growing conviction that native peoples were not only as humane as members of the so-called advanced societies but also every bit as cultured. He entered a tribal world with fine gradations of rank, complex rules of etiquette, and a vast body of legends and symbols that lent beauty and significance to all facets of life. Yet little of this would have been accessible to him without Hunt's assistance and guidance. The Kwakiutl, like neighboring groups, looked upon all their cultural possessions— stories, dances, and carvings—as family heirlooms, to be shared only with one's descendants or with noble guests who were worthy of such privileges. Hunt taught Boas how to demonstrate his nobility to heads of Kwakiutl households by holding a potlatch and distributing presents, thus placing the chiefs in his debt.

The gifts Boas offered at his potlatch were simple enough, amounting in his own words to little more than "hard tack and molasses." But the Kwakiutls then had to demonstrate their own generosity by hosting Boas at their feasts and ceremonies, including the initiation rituals of secret societies, and by lavishing him with gifts and praise. One guest at his potlatch likened Boas to a "loaded canoe that has anchored in front of a mountain from which wealth is rolling down upon all the people of the whole world." This was less a tribute to Boas than to the Kwakiutl, whose leading families piled up hundreds of trade blankets and other goods to give away at potlatches and boasted of burying their rivals under mounds of wealth.

Hunt did more than orchestrate the entry of Boas into Kwakiutl society and interpret for him the ceremonies they attended. He also collected tribal artifacts for Boas, who displayed them at the American Museum of Natural History in New York, where he served as curator. Like other eager collectors of the day, Hunt at times caused offense. Some Kwakiutls complained when he excavated old, untended grave sites and removed artifacts left there as offerings to the dead. On another occasion, he visited the Nootka on the west coast of Vancouver Island and purchased from two chiefs a shrine where whale hunters had long bathed and purified themselves amid sacred carvings. Rumors of the sale so disturbed villagers that the chiefs asked Hunt not to remove the shrine for shipment to New York until the Nootka departed on one of their seasonal migrations. For the most part, however, Hunt's collecting was careful and scrupulous. Despite other duties, including working in a canning factory to help support his family, he fulfilled Boas's request that he detail in writing the significance of the artifacts and the legends associated with them, greatly increasing the value of the collection to posterity.

Boas was by no means the only outsider who relied on Hunt's guidance. Beginning about 1910, Edward Curtis—who had for some time been portraying tribes of the Northwest for his multivolume photographic study *The North American Indian*—set out with Hunt's help to capture the drama of Kwakiutl ceremonies through the new medium of motion pictures. Although the Kwakiutl staged events for Curtis, his films were faithful to tribal tradition in their details, thanks in large part to Hunt, who either gathered existing artifacts to serve as props or obtained accurate reproductions. Indeed, Hunt himself carved one of the totem poles that appeared on film.

Franz Boas once declared to the Kwakiutl that he hoped his "friend, George Hunt, would become the storage box of your laws and of your stories." Like others across the continent who worked to preserve their tribal heritage, Hunt became that and something more—an expert interpreter who helped convey the richness of his culture to others.

~PICTURES~
OF THE KIOWA

Horace Monroe Poolaw, 1979

When Horace Poolaw died in 1986 at age 78, he left behind photographs of his fellow Kiowas spanning more than 50 years. His love of the visual image began when he was a boy in Mountain View, Oklahoma. At age 15, he bought his first camera and began studying photography by correspondence. Apprenticed in the 1920s, Poolaw learned the trade so well that during World War II he taught aerial photography in the Army Air Corps. But economic conditions kept him from parlaying his passion into a career, and to make ends meet, he worked as a farmer and rancher. In 1990 Stanford University exhibited Poolaw's works, including some negatives he was never able to print. "He did not want to be remembered himself," said his daughter Linda. "He wanted his people to remember themselves through his pictures."

The Poolaw homestead, ca. 1929

Poolaw's father, George, who served as a U.S. Cavalry scout in the late 1800s, sits with his grandson Jerry and daughter-in-law Lucy next to the sweat lodge in the family backyard in Mountain View, Oklahoma. Poolaw's kinspeople and friends were the primary subjects of his photographs.

Nieces and nephews, ca. 1928

George Poolaw, arrow maker, ca. 1929

"The Ada No. 1," ca. 1930

This oil well was dug on Indian land in Binger, Oklahoma. "Some of our people got lucky and found oil on their allotments," Poolaw's wife, Winnie, recalled. "I remember one called the Ada No. 1. I was glad it was a Caddo Indian well because all my brothers and sisters are part Caddo."

Camping: Pawnee, Oklahoma, ca. 1929

Poolaw family members on an outing to attend Pawnee Bill's Indian and Wild
West Show relax in their camp tent between performances.

Poolaw cousins, ca. 1928

After the peyote meeting, ca. 1930

Kiowa Peyotists gather outside the ceremonial tipi in the early morning after a
sacred service. "My father was welcome at every event," Poolaw's daughter Linda recalled.
"He respected all his people's choices in their ways of praising the Creator."

The Carnegie, Oklahoma, baseball team, ca. 1933

Lizzie Little Joe, 1955

Funeral of Mrs. Able Big Bow, ca. 1950

Prize-winning canners, Craterville Fair, ca. 1929

Comanche troupe, Craterville Fair, ca. 1928

Comanche participants pose in regalia. Kiowas and Kiowa Apaches also took part in the two-week-long event that featured dances, horse races, and footraces.

Indian princesses on parade, 1941

Mudmen on parade, 1941

Caked with red mud and riding in a wagon filled with willow branches, "mudmen" roll
through Anadarko, Oklahoma, during the American Indian Exposition. "They would scare young children,"
Linda Poolaw recalled. "Every child would wait every single year for the mudmen."

THE PAINTER'S VISION

"I wanted to tell, with paint, brush, and paper, the way of my people," explains Pablita Velarde, one of the first Native American women to take up a career in painting. Velarde's goal has been pursued by the other influential contemporary Indian artists whose paintings appear on these pages. Each has a different tale to tell—about timeless ceremonies and symbols, as well as about daily life. By mixing elements of both traditional Indian and European styles, these artists remain faithful to the past without being bound by it. It is not the portrayal of Indian scenes that makes their work "Indian" but rather the conviction that underlies each creation. As one scholar has noted, modern Indian art is "about survival—the survival of the spirit."

KOSHARES OF TAOS

HER FIRST DANCE

Pablita Velarde

Although she defied Pueblo tradition by becoming an artist when only men were expected to paint, Pablita Velarde has devoted herself to depicting the ways of her people. Born in Santa Clara Pueblo in 1918, Velarde has drawn on her own experiences and the stories of her grandparents to create her "memory paintings," rich in historical detail. Her art embodies the strength of Pueblo cultural identity.

SOUTHERN CHEYENNE SUN DANCE

WHEEL PLAYERS

W. Richard West

One of the deans of traditional Indian painting, West has never forgotten his roots among the Cheyenne people of the southern Plains. He documents their lives and legends in his unique style. "There will always be Indian art because of the color of skin. But without exposure to the old culture," West warns, "it's like a non-Indian trying to paint Indian."

CHEYENNE WINTER GAMES

WOMAN AND BLUEBERRIES

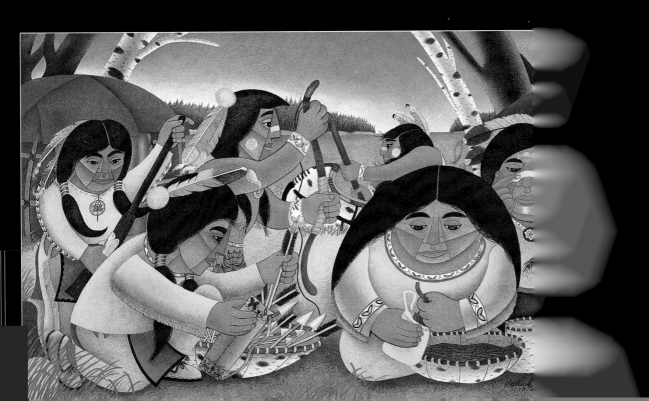

RED LAKE FISHERMEN

Patrick DesJarlait

Growing up on the shores of Red Lake in northwestern Minnesota, Patrick DesJarlait was constantly aware of the presence of the lake, and he later brought that presence into his art. The lake supplied food, livelihood, transportation, and a spiritual focus for his people, the Red Lake Ojibwa (Chippewa). "Each of my paintings tells a story about some aspect of Chippewa life," DesJarlait said before he died in 1973. "It has always been my hope that my paintings will help remind my people of their own heritage."

TWO GUNS ARIKARA

BEEF ISSUE AT FORT SILL

COYOTE KOSHARES WITH WATERMELON

COYOTE DANCER

Harry Fonseca

"In order for a myth to stay alive, it has to change with the times," says Harry Fonseca. Intrigued by the Coyote stories of his Maidu ancestors, Fonseca delights in placing this mythological trickster into modern settings. "At times, Coyote is very playful and foolish," Fonseca explains. "However, I never forget he is wild, that he can bite very, very hard; he is a survivor."

COYOTE AND ROSE DOIN' IT AT INDIAN MARKET WITH A LITTLE HELP FROM GAIL, YAZZIE, AND JODY

3

VOICES FROM THE HOMELANDS

Stretched out on a hide, a Pueblo youth listens intently to the tale told by his elder in the photograph opposite, taken about 1910. Indian writers such as Charles Eastman of the Dakota Sioux have drawn inspiration from ancient tribal traditions of storytelling and wisdom keeping.

On May 15, 1931, more than 200 people gathered on the Pine Ridge Reservation in South Dakota at the home of the Lakota Sioux holy man Black Elk for a feast that welcomed into the tribal circle John G. Neihardt, a poet who had come there to commit Black Elk's story to writing. For Lakotas, who had suffered many indignities at the hands of outsiders, embracing a white man like Neihardt was an act of great goodwill, and the poet repaid the favor in part by purchasing a whole bull for the feast. Men prepared the animal as they had buffalo in the past, savoring the liver raw and reserving other parts for a stew, to be cooked in the bull's paunch. Guests came dressed for the occasion in their ceremonial best—some in beaded shirts and buckskins, and the older men in war bonnets that evoked days long past but not forgotten.

Before feasting, the old warriors formed a circle of honor in ancestral fashion and recounted their exploits to the pounding of drums. One Lakota named Standing Bear told of fighting federal troops at the Little Bighorn in 1876 and shooting a soldier who emerged like a ghost from the pall of dust and smoke cloaking the battlefield. Another told of rescuing a blind Lakota who had been seized by a rival party of Crow warriors. But the last and most compelling story came from Black Elk himself, and it lent a mournful note to the proceedings.

Black Elk spoke of a tragic event that remained fresh in the memories of his listeners more than four decades later—the massacre at Wounded Knee Creek of hundreds of Lakotas by federal troops sent to detain and disarm them in December 1890. Black Elk, then in his mid-twenties, had not been among the party attacked at Wounded Knee. But he had sympathized with their devotion to the Ghost Dance—a ritual that promised divine redemption for Indians and ruin for whites, so unnerving federal authorities that they used deadly force to suppress it. When Black Elk heard that trouble was brewing at Wounded Knee, he hurried to the scene, only to find that the slaughter had already begun. "Soldiers were standing there mowing the women and children down," he related. "There I stood and cried."

"Almost every evening a myth, or a true story of some deed done in the past, was narrated by one of the parents or grandparents, while the boy listened with parted lips and glistening eyes."

CHARLES EASTMAN, DAKOTA SIOUX

Intent on defending his people, Black Elk joined other men on a hilltop overlooking the creek in a desperate charge aimed at distracting the troops and affording Lakotas who were pinned down a chance to escape. True to his calling as a holy man, Black Elk advanced without a weapon, trusting in spirit powers he communed with in dreams to protect him. "I depended on my vision," he explained to those in the circle, "and so I went down and showed the soldiers what power I had." Such daring had long been demonstrated in battle by devout Lakotas who ran at the enemy to show their faith in spirits called *heyoka*—awesome thunder beings who emboldened young men and shielded them. But no medicine of the Lakota was proof against the hail of fire unleashed at Wounded Knee by soldiers wielding repeating rifles and Gatling guns. For all their courage, Black Elk and the others were driven back, and the slaughter continued. He had come up against a destructive force that could not be deflected by spirit power alone. "It was hopeless," he confided. "So I decided to take it just as it was. It was

On the Pine Ridge Reservation in South Dakota in May 1931, poet John G. Neihardt (left) sits beside the Lakota holy man Black Elk (center) and his friend Standing Bear, in a picture taken by Neihardt's daughter Hilda, during interviews for the book "Black Elk Speaks."

BLACK ELK SPEAKS

Being the Life Story of a Holy
Man of the Ogalala Sioux

AS TOLD TO

JOHN G. NEIHARDT

(Flaming Rainbow)

Illustrated by STANDING BEAR

NEW YORK ▼ MCMXXXII
WILLIAM MORROW & COMPANY

The title page for the first edition of
"Black Elk Speaks," published in 1932,
features illustrations by Standing Bear.
Neihardt, who received the name Flaming
Rainbow from Black Elk, based the text
on transcriptions of the interviews.

a butchering, and I cried because I couldn't defend my people in time."

It said much about Black Elk that in a setting where others celebrated their triumphs, he spoke of adversity and heartbreak. He still trusted in the spirits and the visions they imparted to him, and he prayed that the "sacred hoop" of the Lakota—the communal circle of pride and hope that had been shattered at Wounded Knee—would one day be mended. But he could not ignore the cruel setbacks his people had suffered in his lifetime, and he confronted that sad history "just as it was." By facing the bitter reality of defeat without losing faith, Black Elk redefined bravery, not simply for Lakotas but for members of other tribal groups who had undergone similar ordeals in recent times.

Whites, as well, lamented the wrongs done to Indians and wondered how to preserve their own visions and ideals in a world of strife and intolerance. John Neihardt, for one, regarded Black Elk as a prophet for all Americans. The two had first met in August 1930, while Neihardt was interviewing Lakotas for a poem he was writing about the Ghost Dance movement and Wounded Knee. Informed that there was a holy man at Pine Ridge who had witnessed the massacre, Neihardt made his way down a "dead-end road that led through the treeless, yellow hills to Black Elk's home—a one-room log cabin with weeds growing out of the dirt roof." To Neihardt, it seemed that nothing much ever changed in that country. "There was little for the old men to do," he wrote, "but wait for yesterday."

Yet Black Elk appeared to be anticipating the arrival of someone who could convey his insights to others, and he seized the opportunity that

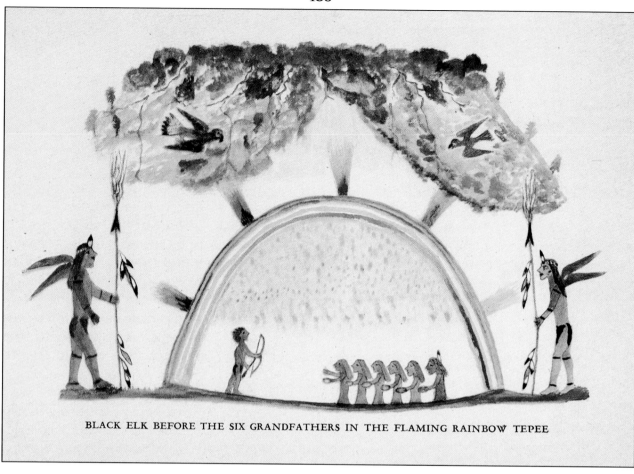

BLACK ELK BEFORE THE SIX GRANDFATHERS IN THE FLAMING RAINBOW TEPEE

Neihardt presented. Some 30 years earlier, after pondering the bitter lessons of Wounded Knee and realizing that life had changed irrevocably for the Lakota, Black Elk had accepted Catholicism and worked to convert hundreds of Indians to that faith. Now he had grown old and nearly blind, however, and before he died he wanted to share with the world those haunting visions of spirit power that had come to him in his youth and that still held profound significance for him.

At their first meeting, Black Elk recognized Neihardt as someone who could be trusted with those revelations. "As I sit here," he said to the friend who translated his remarks for Neihardt, "I can feel in this man beside me a strong desire to know the things of the Other World. He has been sent to learn what I know, and I will teach him." When Neihardt returned in 1931 to learn more from Black Elk and transform his teachings into a book, the 67-year-old holy man felt the need to adopt the 50-year-old poet—or "vision teller," as Black Elk called him—much as other Indians had earlier adopted captives and ethnographers before imparting to them the deeper secrets of their culture. The feast Black Elk hosted for Neihardt in May served as the occasion for an initiation rite, or naming ceremony, which took place atop a hill shortly after Black Elk spoke of his grief at Wounded Knee.

Honored along with Neihardt were his daughters, Hilda and Enid. They accompanied their father to transcribe Black Elk's remarks as trans-

In this illustration by Standing Bear for "Black Elk Speaks," the young Black Elk stands within the rainbow lodge, facing his six grandfathers, during the great vision that came to him as a boy and filled him with spirit power.

lated by his son, Ben, who had learned English at the Carlisle Indian Industrial School in Pennsylvania. Standing with their father, Hilda and Enid were welcomed as Lakotas and given the names Daybreak Star Woman and She Walks with Her Sacred Stick, respectively. Neihardt would be addressed by Black Elk thereafter as "son" or "nephew," and would refer to Black Elk as "uncle." But the poet also received a formal title during the ceremony—Flaming Rainbow, a term whose full significance he would appreciate only in days to come, when Black Elk related to him a great vision he had experienced at the age of nine.

That vision was exceptional both in its details and in its circumstances. Many Native Americans embarked on vision quests by fasting, going without sleep, and enduring further hardships that prepared them to leave the visible world and commune with divine powers. Black Elk sometimes pursued inspiration in that way, but his first great vision came as an unsolicited gift from the spirits, who sought him out as a boy when he was felled by an illness that left him paralyzed. As he lay near death, he heard men calling to him from the clouds—voices he had heard before when he was out walking on his own. This time, the spirit messengers summoned him with irresistible words: "Hurry! Come! Your grandfathers are calling you!"

Black Elk left his ailing body and followed the messengers up into the clouds. "When I looked down I could see my mother and my father yonder," he related, "and I felt sorry to be leaving them." Amid the clouds, Black Elk saw horses all around—black ones to the west, white ones to the north, sorrels to the east, and buckskins to the south. A bay horse came alongside Black Elk and led him to where the clouds rose to a peak like a tipi. At the entrance to that heavenly lodge stood a rainbow, and Black Elk passed under it. Within, he encountered his grandfathers—six old men, sitting in council.

For the Lakota as for the Zuni and other native peoples, the universe had six directions or regions—east and west, north and south, the sky above, and the earth below. Each of the grandfathers in Black Elk's vision embodied one of those regions and the sacred medicine that was associated with it. The first grandfather represented the west and the ferocity of approaching storms; he gave Black Elk a bow and arrow and the fury of the thunder beings in warfare. The second grandfather embodied the north and empowered Black Elk to banish sickness and hardship and lift people's hearts as the geese did when they flew north at winter's end. The third represented the east and the rising sun and offered the boy a pipe of peace and healing. The fourth personified the south in all its warmth and fertility and gave Black Elk a red stick that bloomed at one end and had the capacity to renew the earth. The fifth represented the Great Spirit above and changed into an eagle before Black Elk's eyes, inspiring him to soar high in his dreams and see beyond the horizon.

The sixth grandfather embodied the earth—the realm Black Elk had come from and to which he would soon return. "You shall have my power in going back to the earth," the old man promised him. "Your nation on earth shall have great difficulties. There you shall go." The sixth grandfather then walked out through the rainbow, and as the boy followed, he could see his grandfather rejuvenating and taking on Black Elk's own features: "At the first he was an old man but he got younger and younger until he was a little boy nine years old."

Lone Buffalo, an Omaha elder on the tribe's reservation in Nebraska, records a corn song on a wax cylinder in August 1905. Such recordings helped preserve the riches of the Native American oral tradition.

There was more to Black Elk's vision—ordeals that foretold the difficult road that lay ahead for him and his people—but in the end he returned to earth and to life, as the sixth grandfather assured him he would. Before departing, he saw the rainbow flaming in the clouds, radiating the truths he had received. Then he felt an eagle hovering over him and guiding him home. "No one was with me then but the eagle," he recalled, "but I knew that I was coming back to the center of the nation's hoop." Reentering his family's lodge, he saw a boy "lying there dying" and stared at the youth for some time before he recognized himself and became that child again. "The boy is feeling better now," he heard someone say. Looking up, he saw his mother and father leaning over him. "They were giving me some medicine," he related, "but it was not that that cured me—it was my vision that cured me."

The imparting of Black Elk's great vision to Neihardt exemplified an age-old Native American tradition of wisdom keeping, in which elders drew on the lessons of a lifetime and bequeathed the power of understanding to future generations. Black Elk's vision reflected teachings he absorbed early on from his elders—including his father and grandfather, both of whom were medicine men—and the experience of his later years that allowed him to make sense of the dream and share it with others. As he did so, he felt the power of his revelation leave him and enter those receiving it. "Now I have given you my vision," he told Neihardt, "and with it I have given you my power." But he trusted that his wisdom would thus be preserved and passed on to others.

In blessing Neihardt with the name Flaming Rainbow, Black Elk invited the poet to serve as the gateway for his vision and diffuse its radiance to people far beyond the hoop of the Lakota. To reinforce that point, Black Elk gave Neihardt a splendid gift—a tipi painted with a flaming rainbow above the entryway. Neihardt and his daughters slept there before and after the feast, as Black Elk unfolded his vision and drew them into the sacred circle.

The tipi painting was not the only artistic reflection of Black Elk's teachings. His old friend Standing Bear, who was one of several other Lakotas interviewed by Neihardt for the book, provided paintings for the first edition of *Black Elk Speaks,* a work that attracted only a small audience when it appeared in 1932 but that endured to become one of the most influential Native American narratives.

In illustrating Black Elk's account, Standing Bear was honoring another longstanding tribal tradition—that of painting pictures to reinforce the oral record of a crucial event or revelation. Pictures and words often went hand in hand when Indians recounted their history. The Iroquois, for example, used the beaded designs on their wampum belts as aids in memorizing and relating the sequence of events in council deliberations and treaty talks. Tribes of the Northwest Coast, for their part, could look to the totem poles at the entryway to their great houses and relate in fabulous detail how the spirits portrayed there had revealed themselves in the mythical past and bequeathed their powers to the family residing within. The stories tribespeople told were often rendered all the more dramatic through song and dance. Indian chroniclers were consummate performers, who made the past present and brought the lessons of history home.

Not all storytellers required the accompaniment of music, gestures, or pictures to make a lasting impression, however. Steeped in the rich oral tradition that flourished in native societies without written languages, the best Indian chroniclers boasted prodigious memories and could enchant listeners with the sheer volume and precision of their recollections. Such powers of recall made some Native Americans expert linguists. Often, when Europeans and Indians came together as strangers, it was native speakers who first crossed the language barrier and learned enough of the white man's talk to serve as interpreters. Once they had command of spoken English, many Indians learned to read and write the language as well.

Station manager Patsy Apachito broadcasts from the studio of KABR on the Alamo Navajo Reservation in New Mexico. With programs in English and Navajo reaching more than 10,000 people, KABR is one of many Indian radio stations working to perpetuate native languages and lore.

As English proliferated in tribal communities, native dialects sometimes withered. But tribal chroniclers gained something of real value in exchange—a common language and access to the power of the printed word. Writing in English became a means for Indians of diverse backgrounds to articulate their shared heritage and to convey that heritage directly to others without relying on intermediaries.

For chroniclers like Black Elk, who could neither speak English nor write it, collaborators like Neihardt would continue to play a vital role in communicating their stories to outsiders. Neihardt was mistaken, however, when he ventured enthusiastically that *Black Elk Speaks* would be the "first absolutely Indian book." The book was indeed inspired by Black Elk and true to his vision, but Neihardt contributed to it as an editor and poetic interpreter. Furthermore, Indians had been writing their own books in English for more than a century and, in the process, transforming their powerful oral tradition into literature.

The first American Indian known to have written a book about his life was William Apess, a Pequot born in Massachusetts in 1798. His autobiography *A Son of the Forest,* published in 1829, was in one sense a story of assimilation, relating his upbringing by whites and his conversion to Christianity and the ministry. Far from losing his native identity, however, Apess emerged as a bold Indian prophet who challenged white assumptions of superiority and spoke for other tribal peoples, anticipating the pan-Indian movement of the 20th century.

His troubled childhood typified the plight of his fellow Pequots, who still lived under the shadow of a brutal defeat inflicted on them by English colonists in the 17th century. Like neighboring Algonquian groups, the small number of Pequots who survived the conflict were relegated to tiny reservations or dismal shantytowns, where the strong ties that once held native families together were frayed by poverty and alcoholism—a condition whites promoted by offering Indians strong drink to lure them aboard ships or into brothels or simply to deprive them of their meager earnings.

Crafted by potter Helen Cordero of Cochiti Pueblo in the 1960s, this figure portrays a storyteller regaling a bevy of youngsters. Influenced by earlier Pueblo potters, Cordero in turn inspired artists who followed her to mold their own storyteller figures.

William Apess's parents separated when he was about three years old and left him in the unsteady hands of his maternal grandparents. Once, he related, after his grandmother had been out selling "baskets and brooms" and squandered her cash on rum, she returned in a rage and beat him so severely that she broke his arm "into three pieces." Such violence defied the traditions of her people, who had always treated children gently. Looking back, Apess traced his grandmother's misdeeds not to the innate cruelty that whites wrongly attributed to Indians but to the degradation visited on his people since colonial times. "No such sufferings were heard of, or known among our people," he wrote, "until the burning curse and demon of despair came among us."

When young William's plight came to the attention of authorities, they took him from his grandparents and indentured him as a servant to a white man named Furman, who afforded him a basic education but otherwise mistreated him. Once when the boy was ill, Furman tried to beat the "devil" out of him with a cane. True to his heritage, William resisted all such coercive lessons or "cures." He ultimately found great discipline, but it came not from elders who threatened him but from those who instructed him with wise words and good examples, as Indian teachers had been doing for ages. His first such advice came from his master's wife, the "good Mrs. Furman," who offered him moral encouragement that had more effect on him than "40 floggings." But William lost her counsel when Furman sold him for $20 to another man, who in turn peddled him to a third overseer a few months later.

Dismayed at being treated like property, William longed for a family that would offer him guidance and devotion. He found such acceptance among a group that rival Protestants derided as "noisy Methodists" for their loud professions of faith and fervent hymn singing. Like other revivalists of the day, they believed in communing directly with the Holy Ghost and praising that power in words and song—an approach that harmonized with William's inherited beliefs. The conversion experience he underwent at the age of 15, for example, was not unlike a vision quest. For many nights, he found it hard to sleep and fancied that "evil spirits stood around my bed." One evening as he dozed, he had a frightful vision of hell, a "world of fire . . . red and glowing with heat," after which he journeyed in his dream to a land of redemption, where everyone was at peace: "Oh, how I longed to be among that happy company. I sighed to be free from misery and pain." Shortly thereafter, his prayers were answered, and he embraced God with such joy and conviction "that I could praise him aloud even in my sleep."

His guardian at the time was a strict Presbyterian who forbade him to attend Methodist meetings because he was "too young to be religiously inclined." He was not too young by his own standards, however, for the transition from childhood to adulthood was a time of spiritual decision for Indians. He expressed his conviction by continuing to meet covertly with the Methodists, whose preachers delighted him by dispensing with prepared texts and speaking as moved by the "power of the Holy Ghost." Although he learned to express himself forcefully in writing, he retained the profound respect of his ancestors for the spoken truth and a corresponding aversion to curses and profanity.

William Apess did not move swiftly or easily from his conversion to his calling as a minister. After a brief period of religious certainty, he lapsed into doubt. In the fall of 1813, while still only 15, he joined the army and fought against the British along the Canadian border. Afterward, he lived for some time in Canada and worked at various tasks and trades before returning to his homeland about the age of 19 and rediscovering his faith. Most young Anglo-Americans bound for the ministry followed a straighter path. But his odyssey was altogether fitting for an Indian prophet. For him as for Black Elk, the trials of warfare and the loneliness of exile equipped the holy man to speak for his people with greater compassion and authority.

As a preacher, Apess wanted to serve Indians and stir the conscience of whites. In 1833 those objectives came together when he went to Mashpee, Massachusetts, a tribal reserve on Cape Cod established in the 1600s as a "praying town" for Christian Indians. The state overseers who governed the Mashpee cared less for their rights than for the interests of neighboring whites, who were allowed to graze cattle on the reserve and cut

DEPICTING TRIBAL HISTORY

The winter count below documents Lakota history from 1798 to 1912 through pictographs symbolizing a key event for each successive year, beginning at upper left and spiraling inward clockwise. The final entries (center) record the appearance of Halley's comet in 1910 and an epidemic of measles two years later.

"A people without history is like wind on the buffalo grass." That saying of the Sioux expresses the universal determination of tribal peoples to preserve a record of their past. Lacking written languages, native chroniclers of the Plains used pictographs to denote a significant event for each year on their winter counts—so called because the keeper of the count added a new symbol to the hide every winter to represent the preceding year. Those revealing calendars, supplemented by the stories told by elders, helped youngsters envision the experiences of earlier generations and learn the lessons of history.

Indians have been recording their traditions pictorially for thousands of years.

The ancient rock art that endures in many parts of North America testifies to the long and intimate relationship between native hunters and their prey. The first Americans may well have portrayed the animals on which they depended for survival as a way of appealing to those creatures spiritually and ensuring a bountiful hunt. In more recent times, Indian artists continued to devote great effort and skill to depicting the close bonds between humans and animals, sometimes inscribing hunting rituals or scenes of the chase on bones, hide, or other materials derived from their prey.

For Indian chroniclers, such moments were as important as battles or peace councils. Renderings of rituals, ceremonies, and legends were all part of a tribe's sacred history, which revealed how people acquired blessings from ancestral spirits and renewed those gifts from season to season.

Crafted in northern Alaska, this Inuit carving depicts a walrus hunt on the jawbone of a beluga whale—another creature that the Inuit hunted with much ceremony.

Hunters armed with bows target bighorn sheep in rock carvings made by Indians in California at least 1,500 years ago. Introduction of the bow and arrow may have contributed to the demise of bighorn sheep in the area and caused hunters to wonder if they had offended the animal's spirit.

In a scene painted on deer hide by Indians of the Great Lakes area, dancers participating in a ceremony of a mysterious nature hold a rattle in one hand and a feathered staff in the other (shown in detail, inset).

Garsventre Indians in council.

This inscribed birch-bark container, designed in the 19th century by a member of Maine's Passamaquoddy tribe, shows a hunter at his campsite, confronting a bear.

in Illustrations
at Crow Agency M.T 1883

An 1883 northern Plains ledger drawing portrays
Gros Ventre Indians attending a council meeting at the Crow Agency in Montana. Lacking
buffalo hides, artists on reservations continued
to chronicle important events in ledger books.

A lofty totem pole carved
for a 19th-century chief of
the Tsimshian tribe in
British Columbia honors
his spiritual ancestors—
legendary figures who be-
queathed their powers to
his noble household.

wood there—a scarce commodity on Cape Cod. To make matters worse, a Congregational minister appointed by Harvard College alienated the Mashpee by reading his sermons in rote fashion and refusing to allow a popular Baptist preacher from their own ranks, Blind Joe Amos, to conduct services in their Old Indian Meeting House.

Apess abhorred such outside interference in the Indians' affairs and helped organize resistance among the Mashpee, who petitioned Harvard to remove the offending minister and addressed to the governor of Massachusetts an "Indian Declaration of Independence," which insisted that "we, as a tribe, will rule ourselves, and have the right to do so; for all men are born free and equal, says the Constitution of the country." Apess backed up those words with action on July 1 when he led Mashpees in preventing whites from cutting wood on the reserve. On July 4, he was arrested for his part in this so-called Mashpee Revolt, sentenced to 30 days in prison, and fined $100, a steep penalty in those days. He used his newfound notoriety to appeal through the press to the public on behalf of the Mashpee, likening their plight to that of the Cherokee and other southern tribes who had recently been evicted from homelands guaranteed them by treaty. "Perhaps you have heard of the oppression of the Cherokees and lamented over them much, and thought the Georgians were hard and cruel creatures," he declared. "But did you ever hear of the poor, oppressed and degraded Mashpee Indians in Massachusetts, and lament over them?"

Such protests from Apess, combined with appeals by Mashpees, helped persuade state legislators to recognize the reserve as a self-governing township. Later, Mashpees forced out the unpopular Congregational minister. For Apess, the revolt was part of a larger campaign to assert the civil and religious rights of Indians. He charted a path for future advocates of Native American sovereignty, both in his defense of the Mashpee and in a remarkable address he delivered in Boston in 1836 and published the same year. Entitled *Eulogy on King Philip,* it constituted one of the first efforts to reinterpret American history from a native perspective and to change the way whites perceived Indians.

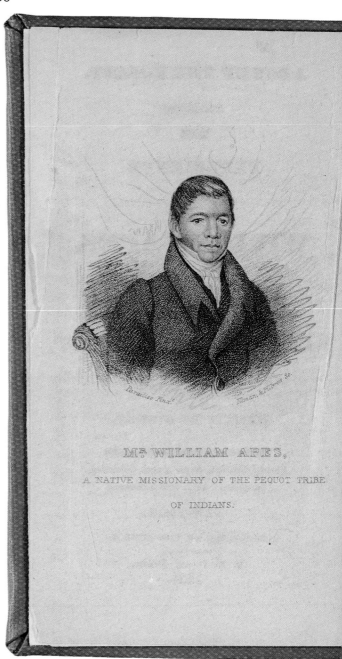

Pictured here in the second edition of his autobiography "A Son of the Forest," the author, a Pequot from Massachusetts, changed the spelling of his name from Apes to Apess in later publications.

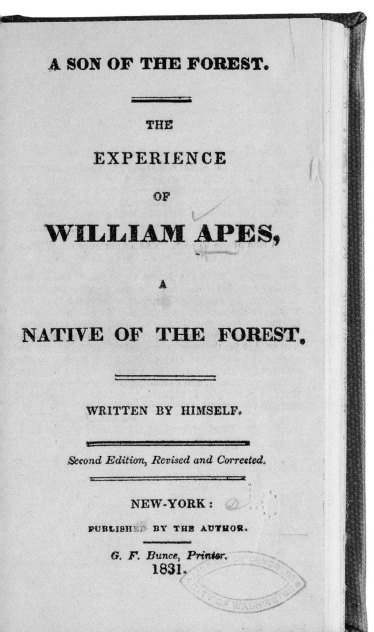

A SON OF THE FOREST.

THE

EXPERIENCE

OF

WILLIAM APES,

A

NATIVE OF THE FOREST.

WRITTEN BY HIMSELF.

Second Edition, Revised and Corrected.

NEW-YORK:

PUBLISHED BY THE AUTHOR.

G. F. Bunce, Printer.
1831.

Apess argued forcefully that the Wampanoag chief known as Metacomet, or King Philip, in leading his own tribe and allied groups against the English in 1675, was a patriot in the mold of George Washington and other heroes of the American Revolution. Indeed, Philip's cause was even stronger than theirs because his people had never been English subjects, yet were treated worse than the lowliest colonists. Although his father, Chief Massasoit, had made a pact with the colonists as an independent power, colonial leaders repeatedly violated Philip's sovereignty. In one case, they required him to surrender his warriors' arms and ammunition, a demand Anglo-Americans would never have tolerated from outside authorities. Apess proudly cited Philip's reply when emissaries sought belatedly to appease him by inviting him to talks with the colonial governor of Massachusetts. "Your governor is but a subject of King Charles of England," Philip responded. "I shall not treat with a subject; I shall treat of peace only with a king, my brother; when he comes, I am ready."

Although Philip and his followers were defeated, Apess rejected the Puritan notion that the outcome was ordained by God and that whites had a divine right to displace Indians. Such an attitude was blasphemous, he insisted, for it ascribed to a just and merciful God actions rooted in human malice. For too long, pious whites had prayed for the ruin of Indians and thanked Providence when those appeals were seemingly answered. "If this is the way they pray," Apess declared, "I hope they will not pray for me; I should rather be excused."

He was grimly prophetic in recognizing that whites intent on mastering other races would not soon divest themselves of the belief that God had openly condemned Indians, Africans, and others by cursing them with dark skin—a condition that Apess himself regarded as a blessing. He could still hear whites praising God for their own ungodly deeds, much as the militant Puritans had: "I do not hesitate to say that through the prayers, preaching, and examples of those pretended pious has been the foundation of all the slavery and degradation in the American colonies toward colored people."

Apess tempered his indignation with appeals to the higher principles of the descendants of the Puritans in his audience, employing his knowledge of their spiritual vocabulary to win them over. He concluded his address with an entreaty that he described humbly as the wish of a "poor Indian," asking for reconciliation. "You and I have to rejoice that we have not to answer for our fathers' crimes," he told his listeners. "Neither shall we do right to charge them to another." The only solution, he concluded, was for both sides to renounce the sins of the fathers and "henceforth, let peace and righteousness be written upon our hearts and hands forever."

When he mastered English, William Apess acquired a tool that helped him influence both whites and members of various eastern tribes who grew up near Anglo-Americans and learned their language. Among western tribes, however, most Indians as yet had little communication with whites. Those few who became literate in English often served as intermediaries between their people and outside authorities. Such was the case with Sarah Winnemucca of Nevada's Northern Paiutes. Her autobiography, published in 1883, was part of a wider effort on her part to make the hopes and sorrows of Paiutes understandable to whites and appeal to them for compassion and justice.

That diplomatic role was not easy for her to assume, because she grew up in an atmosphere of rising tension between Paiutes and intruding whites. From early childhood, she was torn between fear of the intruders and the expectation of her elders—notably her maternal grandfather, Captain Truckee—that she would follow their lead in reaching out to Anglo-Americans. Captain Truckee earned that title in 1844, about the time of her birth, when he and other Paiutes of his band near Pyramid Lake welcomed explorer John Charles Frémont with the greeting *truckee,* meaning "good." Captain Truckee later traveled with Frémont to California to aid the Americans in gaining control of that territory during the Mexican War and returned with a document certifying him as an American ally. He explained to young Sarah that this paper "talked for him" to the Americans. "Just as long as I live and have that paper," he declared, "I shall stand by them." For Sarah, it was an early lesson in the power of the written word, for the paper commanded respect from whites who might otherwise have been hostile.

Despite Captain Truckee's policy of friendship, Northern Paiutes came to dread Anglo-Americans in the late 1840s when reports of gold and other bounty in California drew whites across their land in ever-increasing numbers. Westward-bound emigrants attacked Indians they perceived as threatening and even targeted some who were friendly to them. In one grim instance, during the winter of 1846-1847, members of the ill-fated Donner party stranded by snow in the Sierra Nevada not only ate the flesh of their white companions who perished but also murdered and cannibalized their two Indian guides. Sarah was warned by her mother afterward that the "whites were killing everybody and eating them." Her people took refuge in the hills, away from the emigrant path, but she and her siblings feared that the white cannibals were coming every time they saw dust "blowing in the valley."

About 1854 Captain Truckee insisted that Sarah and other members of her family join him on a trip to California, where they would see for themselves the virtues of the maligned whites. When she first saw white men close up, with their bearded faces and staring eyes, they looked to her like owls—creatures that many native peoples dreaded as harbingers of evil. "I imagined I could see their big white eyes all night," Sarah wrote. In time she lost her aversion, however, largely as a result of a dreamlike experience that came to her while she was suffering a severe reaction to poison oak. "My face swelled so that I could not see for a long time," she recalled, "but I could hear everything." As she lay blinded, she was approached by someone with a "voice like an angel." She had been told that angels carried dying souls to the spirit land, but this one brought compassion and healing. Afterward, she learned that the "angel" was a white woman who had soothed her with medicine. She concluded that whites possessed power for good as well as for evil and began to view them more as her grandfather did.

Sarah grew closer to whites during the years to come, when her father, Old Winnemucca, who succeeded Captain Truckee as chief of the Paiutes around Pyramid Lake, entrusted her and her sister Elma to the family of Major William Ormsby, a leader of the Americans who were beginning to settle in Nevada. Sarah became one of the few Paiutes of her generation who could read and write English. That proficiency, and the diplomatic skills she learned from her elders, made her a vital link between white authorities and the increasingly beleaguered Paiutes. The discovery of silver in the hills of western Nevada in the late 1850s brought thousands of prospectors to the region and triggered bitter fighting around Pyramid Lake that cost the lives of Major Ormsby and other whites and ended with devastating reprisals against Paiutes.

In the aftermath, Paiutes who had long subsisted by hunting and gathering across a wide area were pressed onto small reservations where they had little chance of succeeding as farmers, as the government directed. When tensions mounted and conflict loomed, both whites and Indians looked to Sarah Winnemucca as a mediator. "Can you speak to them on paper?" Paiutes asked her on one occasion. They watched intently as she translated their spoken appeals into writing, for they knew that papers that "talked" had a peculiar authority for whites.

In time, she and other Paiutes of her band gravitated to the Malheur Reservation in southeastern Oregon, where an enlightened agent named Samuel Parrish treated them with uncommon respect. He told them that they would have to work hard digging irrigation ditches and farming the land, but promised that they would be their own bosses. "All you raise is your own to do with as you like," he told them through Sarah, who served as his interpreter. "The reservation is all yours." Unfortunately, Parrish was replaced in 1876 by another agent, William Rinehart, who arrived with a different agenda. His voice quaking with apprehension, Rinehart asked Sarah to inform the Indians that he had been sent there by the "Big Father in Washington" and that the reservation they occupied belonged to the government alone. If they worked the land diligently, he added, he would pay them for their services.

Rinehart's listeners hardly knew what to say. They joked bitterly in their own tongue that perhaps they should ask a boy to respond—the words of a man might frighten the nervous agent to death. But at length, a chief named Egan summed up the feelings of all present. He began by reminding the agent through Sarah that he and the others could not read and thus were lacking in understanding. But his next words made it clear that they had sized up the situation perfectly: "We don't want the Big Father in Washington to fool with us. He sends one man to say one thing and another to say something else. The man who has just left us told us the land was ours, and what we do on it was ours, and you come and say it is government land and not ours."

Egan and the others had little choice but to accept the new regime, but they were further embittered when the pay they were promised was doled out in the form of government issue clothing and rations. Many were so upset that they joined with neighboring Bannocks in a war against whites in 1878. Sarah Winnemucca wanted no part of that uprising. Instead, she served as an interpreter for the army and helped authorities communicate with the "hostile" Paiutes, who were rounded up and

In an 1880 photograph, Sarah Winnemucca stands beside her father, Old Winnemucca; her brother, Natchez (center); and other close acquaintances. Sarah and her kinspeople mediated between their fellow Paiutes and white authorities during the difficult early years of the reservation era.

confined on the Yakima Reservation in Washington State. She blamed their plight on misguided reservation policies and took to the lecture circuit in 1879 to urge that Rinehart be removed as agent at Malheur and that the Paiutes at Yakima be allowed to return there. Rinehart had been appointed in part because he was a devout Christian, and the government believed that Indians would learn virtue and piety from God-fearing agents. But one reporter who heard Winnemucca expound on Rinehart's sins declared that "there was little left of the redoubtable Christian agent when she finished him." For all her eloquence, she was unable to bring about the changes she desired at Malheur.

Her words alone could not alter the course of history, but like William Apess, she shed light on the past—and offered hope for the future—through her fervent speeches and writings. Her memoir *Life among the Piutes: Their Wrongs and Claims,* edited by social reformer Mary Mann, was remarkable not only for its portrait of the failings of the reservation system but also for its loving depiction of the tribal traditions that were imperiled by that system.

Even whites who were sympathetic to Indians still talked loosely of the need to "civilize" reservation dwellers. But Sarah Winnemucca reminded them that for countless generations before whites arrived, Paiutes had maintained orderly and resourceful communities. Such evils as prostitution were unknown in earlier times, she noted. Indeed, Paiute

Maxine Switzler (far left) performs intricate beadwork and Viola Kalama (near left) produces sturdy willow baskets on the Warm Springs Reservation in Oregon. The two women serve as "keepers of the arts" at The Museum at Warm Springs (below) by sharing their knowledge and skills with other members of the reservation community and with visitors.

A HERITAGE SHARED

Since it opened in March 1993, The Museum at Warm Springs has served as a cultural center for the reservation's three confederated tribes—Warm Springs, Paiute, and Wasco. The museum houses more than 2,000 artifacts and 2,500 photographs, and offers multimedia exhibits that tell of the diverse tribal cultures that were pressed together at Warm Springs in the 19th century and found common ground there.

Seeing their heritage threatened by the sale of traditional artifacts to outside collectors, the council representing all three tribes began in the 1970s to set aside $50,000 from their budget annually to purchase their own collection. Explains Delvis Heath, president of the museum board: "We could see that the old ways were disappearing, the old language was disappearing, and that pretty soon none of our young people would know where they came from or who they were. That's when we decided to build a museum." With little federal funding, they raised the money they needed to establish the state's first Native American museum.

Characteristics of each tribe are evident in the building's innovative architecture, which incorporates the lines of a Paiute travois, a Wasco longhouse, and a Warm Springs tipi. Built largely of local materials, the structure resembles an encampment and offers an experience that one tribal member, Rudy Clement, likens to "going to a sweat lodge or a sacred service." In the words of Delbert Frank, former board president, the museum will continue to find new ways to "tell the story of our people."

elders had closely supervised eligible girls and restricted open displays of affection to ceremonies such as the Festival of Flowers, held in the spring when the desert bloomed. On that occasion, the girls, many of whom were known by the names of flowers until they matured, were free to sing and dance with their sweethearts. Sarah herself had been graced with a flower name when she was young—Thocmetony, or shellflower. In recalling the joyous Flower Dance, she told of ancient hopes that decades of adversity had failed to eradicate. "They all go marching along," she wrote of the Flower Dancers, "each girl in turn singing of herself; but she is not a girl anymore—she is a flower singing. She sings of herself, and her sweetheart, dancing along by her side, helps her sing the song she makes. I will repeat what we say of ourselves. 'I, Sarah Winnemucca, am

Warriors in action adorn this late-1800s muslin dress of Sioux design exemplifying the vivid pictorial chronicling that graced possessions of the Plains dwellers.

a shellflower, such as I wear on my dress. My name is Thocmetony. I am so beautiful! Who will come and dance with me while I am so beautiful? Oh, come and be happy with me! I shall be beautiful while the earth lasts.' "

By the dawn of the 20th century, Indians of various tribes across the country had command of the English language and were writing down their stories. Like William Apess and Sarah Winnemucca, these chroniclers tended to be less concerned with meeting the standards of white society than with living up to the examples of their tribal elders, whose tales and examples proved more enlightening for them in the long run than the knowledge gleaned from classrooms and textbooks. Few Indian chroniclers of the period accomplished more within the white educational system—or offered stronger tribute in the end to the wisdom of their native teachers—than Charles Eastman of the Dakota, or Eastern Sioux. Eastman underwent a complex learning process that began in

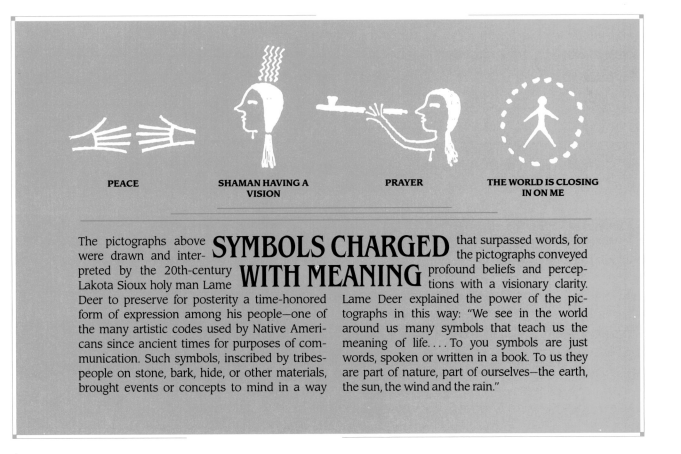

PEACE

SHAMAN HAVING A
VISION

PRAYER

THE WORLD IS CLOSING
IN ON ME

SYMBOLS CHARGED WITH MEANING

The pictographs above were drawn and interpreted by the 20th-century Lakota Sioux holy man Lame Deer to preserve for posterity a time-honored form of expression among his people—one of the many artistic codes used by Native Americans since ancient times for purposes of communication. Such symbols, inscribed by tribespeople on stone, bark, hide, or other materials, brought events or concepts to mind in a way that surpassed words, for the pictographs conveyed profound beliefs and perceptions with a visionary clarity. Lame Deer explained the power of the pictographs in this way: "We see in the world around us many symbols that teach us the meaning of life.... To you symbols are just words, spoken or written in a book. To us they are part of nature, part of ourselves—the earth, the sun, the wind and the rain."

the tribal circle, continued in schools and colleges far from his homeland, and culminated in the realization that the civilization he had become part of was deeply flawed and that he could regain a sense of purpose only by honoring the lessons of his Dakota upbringing.

The grandson of Seth Eastman, a white army officer and artist who married a Dakota woman while stationed at Fort Snelling in Minnesota and later abandoned her, Charles had little contact with whites in his early years. His mixed-blood mother died shortly after giving birth to him in 1858. As the youngest of five children she left behind, he was named Hakadah, or The Pitiful Last. As a young boy, he earned the title Ohiyesa, or Winner, but he did not take the name Eastman until he turned down the white man's path.

In 1862, when Charles was four, his father, Many Lightnings, joined in an uprising against whites sparked by the hardship and mistreatment Dakotas suffered on their reservation in southwestern Minnesota. Many Lightnings was captured and imprisoned for his part in the war, but his son thought he had been executed and grew up longing for retribution. His band fled after the uprising, seeking refuge first in the Dakota Territory and then in Manitoba. Ohiyesa, as Charles was then known, was raised by his uncle and his grandmother, Uncheedah, who together instilled in the boy the virtues of watchfulness and self-control, on which his very survival depended. Before and after their flight, Dakotas were subject to raids by rival tribes, and elders taught children through cautionary tales to be quiet at night so as not to alert enemies. "Do not cry!" Uncheedah would whisper to her grandson when he woke in the dark. "Hinkaga (the owl) is watching you from the treetop." He covered his head and kept still, for Uncheedah had often told him of the boy who was crying for his mother in the night when Hinkaga swooped down and carried him off.

In later years, Ohiyesa learned that the caricature of the "silent Indian" was a source of amusement for whites. But the people who raised him took silence seriously—as an essential trait for hunters and warriors and as a path to wisdom for youngsters, who had to learn to listen before they could speak with any authority. Ohiyesa spent much of his childhood heeding the stories of his elders. At first, he plied them with questions and received polite and informative answers. But as he grew older, he was urged to listen patiently and let speakers have their say. He once interrupted his uncle as he was telling of a fabled woman hunter who crept up on a pair of moose and felled them with two quick draws of her bow. Ohiyesa asked why the animals failed to scent the woman as she approached, for his uncle had

The tipi drawing at top was sketched by Luther Standing Bear of the Lakota to illustrate his book "My People the Sioux." Even the eastern branch of the Sioux—known as the Dakota—lived in hide tipis and hunted on the grasslands for part of the year and delighted in displays of horsemanship like that depicted on the Lakota lodge above.

previously remarked that the moose possessed the "keenest nose" in the forest. "Doubtless the wind was blowing the other way," his uncle replied indulgently. "But, nephew, you must let me finish my story."

Ohiyesa learned to be as intent an observer as he was a listener. Uncheedah taught him which berries, roots, and seeds could be safely eaten and which were to be avoided. She also gathered and administered medicinal plants and encouraged her grandson to follow in her healing path, which he later did as a physician. After she had tutored him in the region's flora, he learned about the fauna from his uncle. "How do you know that there are fish in yonder lake?" Ohiyesa was asked. "Because they jump out of the water for flies at midday," he answered. His uncle smiled at this "prompt but superficial reply" and pointed out other clues, such as the "pretty curved marks" fish made when they brushed the lake's sandy bottom and the presence along the shore of heron and other fish eaters. He urged Ohiyesa to scrutinize his surroundings with the keen deliberation of the wolf, who even in retreat "will pause to take one more look at you. . . . So you must take a second look at everything you see."

The training Ohiyesa received from his kin was reinforced by strong lessons from tribal authorities. Once when his uncle was hunting deer in woods near the Plains, his shots scared away a nearby herd of buffalo, depriving others of a vital resource. Although the offense was accidental, the camp's "soldiers," or police, punished him for his carelessness by destroying his tipi. On another occasion, men of the band encountered some Métis—people of mixed Indian and French Canadian ancestry—and partook of their "spirit water." Several Dakotas came home "crazy and foolish," and their chief ordered them tied up and confined in a lodge until the "evil spirit had gone away." Misdeeds and acts of punishment were rare, however, because Dakotas were taught to curb their impulses and spurn those who failed to do so, such as the fabled young man who murdered a woman in a rage. He paid with his life, and Dakotas disgraced him by covering his corpse with grass. "Control your-

self," Ohiyesa was warned by his grandmother, "or you will be like that young man I told you of, and lie under a *green blanket!*"

From what little he knew of whites, they were a selfish and unruly people, whose leaders treated them with contempt. His uncle informed him that the Great Chief in Washington exacted payment each year from every man "for the land he lives upon and all his personal goods—even for his own existence." And white warriors were evidently so weak in spirit that they had to be "driven forward like a herd of antelopes to face the foe." But the youth was forced to reappraise whites and their ways when he was reunited with his father at the age of 15. During his imprisonment, Many Lightnings had converted to Christianity and taken the name Jacob Eastman. Several years after his release, he went in search of his son and brought the youngster, known thereafter as Charles Eastman, back to Flandreau, in Dakota Territory, where a group of Sioux had taken up farming. "I felt as if I were dead," Charles wrote of that fateful journey, "and traveling to the Spirit Land."

Determined that Charles follow the white man's path, Jacob overcame the boy's resistance to schooling by challenging him as he would a young warrior. Books, Jacob explained, were the "bow and arrows" of the white man. After two years at the mission school at Flandreau, Charles went off to an Indian boarding school in Nebraska. "Remember," his father told him in parting, "it is the same as if I sent you on your first warpath. I shall expect you to conquer."

The trials of boarding school were in some ways worse than those of war because Charles and others in his class entered without command of an essential weapon, written English. "For a whole week we youthful warriors were held up and harassed with words of three letters," he wrote. "Like raspberry bushes in the path, they tore, bled, and sweated us—those little words rat, cat, and so forth—until not a semblance of our native dignity and self-respect was left." No less baffling than reading and writing was the relentless quantification of time and space that his teachers called arithmetic. He had grown up in a world of eternal cycles and inestimable values, but "it seemed now that everything must be measured in time or money or distance."

Drawing on the discipline instilled in him by his tribal teachers, Charles fulfilled his father's ambition that he prove equal to white men "in the ways of the mind." He scored one academic coup after another, graduating from Dartmouth College in 1887 and earning his medical degree from Boston University three years later. By that time, he was 32 years old and fairly

THE EASTMAN LEGACY

Two generations before Charles Eastman chronicled the ways of his Dakota people in writing, his white grandfather, Seth Eastman, recorded their lives on canvas. A soldier who was trained as a draftsman, Eastman used his free time to depict the traditions of Dakotas living near Fort Snelling in Minnesota, where he was stationed twice, first in the early 1830s and again a decade later. Eastman made hundreds of studies in pencil and brush, including the watercolor below, showing a Dakota carrying his new wife off on his shoulders as revelers fire salutes.

Seth Eastman became part of the tribal scene himself when he wed a Dakota woman and fathered a daughter by her, but he left his wife and child when he moved to a new post and never rejoined them. By the time he returned to Fort Snelling in the early 1840s, he had a white wife, Mary Eastman. She too observed Dakota customs closely and wrote a book on the subject. Yet it remained to Charles Eastman, the son of the artist's abandoned daughter, to achieve what eluded Seth and Mary Eastman—a compelling portrait of Dakota culture as seen from the inside.

comfortable in white society. But he was determined to help Indians, and he took on a task that soon caused him to question the values of his adopted culture. He enlisted as a doctor at the Pine Ridge Agency in South Dakota, arriving there in November 1890, less than two months before the massacre at Wounded Knee.

Eastman achieved a rapport with the Lakota Sioux at Pine Ridge by showing respect for their traditions. He once arrived at a lodge to treat a sick child, only to find that a tribal medicine man had been called there as well. Eastman suggested that they "consult together," and they shared a purifying sweat bath. Afterward, the medicine man agreed to the treatment Eastman proposed and visited his office to discuss difficult cases and borrow medicine.

Sadly, Eastman's good work at Pine Ridge was overshadowed by the government's disastrous response to the Ghost Dance movement. Eastman opposed the use of force to suppress the ritual, arguing that the "arrival of troops would be construed by the ghost dancers as a threat or a challenge." That prediction was borne out in late December, when officials sent troops to intercept the Ghost Dance leader Big Foot and his followers, who fled to Pine Ridge from the Cheyenne River Reservation in search of sanctuary among like-minded Lakotas. On December 29 at Wounded Knee, the troops met with resistance as they disarmed Big Foot's anxious followers, and proceeded to massacre them. At the time, Eastman was tending to Lakotas who had flocked to the Pine Ridge Agency in the cold to avoid trouble. But three days later,

Lakotas in ceremonial attire (top) dance in front of Charles Eastman's office on the Pine Ridge Reservation, where Eastman arrived to serve as a physician in November 1890. A man of many interests who valued both the early lessons he absorbed from his Dakota elders and the education he received from whites, Eastman (pictured above in 1918) found himself caught between two worlds.

after a snowstorm, he set out for Wounded Knee to search for survivors.

Eastman's party encountered the first evidence of the tragedy—the lifeless body of a Lakota woman—three miles from Wounded Knee, and from there on they found other scattered victims who had been "hunted down and slaughtered while fleeing for their lives." Reaching Big Foot's campsite, Eastman counted the corpses of 80 men who had been attacked there after "nearly all their guns had been taken from them." Lakotas in the search party cried aloud or sang death songs as they hunted for survivors. Eastman found a year-old baby safely bundled up and brought her back to the agency, where an officer adopted her. Elsewhere on the killing ground, he came upon a mortally wounded Lakota, whose one request was that the doctor fill his pipe. On hills above the creek, where Black Elk and others had launched their diversionary charge during the massacre, Eastman saw warriors keeping a mournful watch.

For him as for Black Elk, Wounded Knee came as a bitter revelation. "All this was a severe ordeal," he confessed, "for one who had so lately put all his faith in the Christian love and lofty ideals of the white man." His disillusionment deepened after the massacre, when he sided with Lakotas who had suffered property losses amid the disruption and were cheated of their full government compensation. Eastman was pressured into resign-

Members of a burial party load the bodies of Lakotas who were massacred by federal troops at Wounded Knee onto a wagon on New Year's Day, 1891. Charles Eastman assumed responsibility for searching among the dead for the few remaining survivors and saving those that he could.

ing his post, and he came away with a growing awareness of what he called the "savagery of civilization." He continued to believe that his people would profit from formal education and inclusion in American society. But he clung with renewed appreciation to the ancestral values his kinspeople had instilled in him. In the years ahead, he celebrated those virtues in writing with the editorial help of his wife, Elaine Goodale, an Anglo-American writer and teacher whom he met at Pine Ridge while she was supervising Indian schools in the vicinity.

Eastman published several books during his lifetime, including two revealing memoirs—*Indian Boyhood* and *From the Deep Woods to Civilization*—as well as *The Soul of the Indian,* a heartfelt celebration of Native American religious and ethical principles. "Long before I ever heard of Christ, or saw a white man," he wrote there in tribute to his grandmother, "I had learned from an untutored woman the essence of morality. With the help of dear Nature herself, she taught me things simple but of mighty import. I knew God. I perceived what goodness is. I saw and loved what is really beautiful. Civilization has not taught me anything better!"

Among the many Indian writers who followed in Charles Eastman's path and drew inspiration from their elders was Christine Quintasket, who took the pen name Mourning Dove. Raised in the late 1800s on Washington State's Colville Reservation, home to the Okanagon and other Interior Salish peoples, she owed much to her many grandmothers, a term she applied to the various elder women who cared for her at home and in her community. As a child, she delighted in family legends concerning her father's grandmother, a fearless medicine woman. Once when traveling with her band, the old woman ventured ahead of the warriors who normally led the way. Nearing a berry patch, she saw a grizzly feeding there and challenged the bear with her sharp digging stick. "You are a mean animal and I am a mean woman," she said to the grizzly. "Let us fight this out to see who will get the berry patch." Growling like a bear, she jabbed her stick repeatedly into the animal's gaping mouth and forced it to retreat, "broken and bleeding."

In an earlier era, Mourning Dove might have emulated her great-grandmother and become one of those exceptional women who rivaled men in deeds of valor. As a girl, she was less interested in playing with dolls than in listening to tales of war and practicing with the bow her father made for her. She had no ambition to marry and go live in her husband's lodge, where she would have to do as told by her mother-in-law. Instead, she dreamed of a home of her own, "where I could have all the grandmothers I wanted to tell me stories."

She was indeed fortunate in having many gifted elder women nearby to learn from as she matured. Prominent among her teachers was an adopted grandmother named Teequalt, who was on her own when Mourning Dove first met her. "Leave me alone," Teequalt said to the child. "I am walking, walking until I die." Mourning Dove ran to her mother and told her that she had found a "new grandmother," who would die if no one cared for her. The family took Teequalt in, and the old woman became the girl's principal tutor and storyteller.

Mourning Dove was encouraged by her mother and Teequalt to seek the spirit medicine that girls as well as boys acquired through vision quests. Like other girls at the onset of puberty, she underwent a 10-day fast in the wild. As part of the ritual, she tied stones under the belt of her dress and let them drop as she scurried up a hillside, reciting as she did so, "When I have children, that is the way they will come, with me on the run." On this and later quests, she learned to brave wandering ghosts and other perils of the night. But no empowering spirits visited her. At length, Teequalt took sacred eagle bones from her medicine bag and gave them to Mourning Dove, who went out that night in search of inspiration from the "chief of birds." Ascending a rocky crag, she could see eagles circling high above in the dawn light, but they kept their distance. "If they did speak to me," she wrote, "they were too far away to hear."

Through such experiences, Mourning Dove learned that her mission in life was not to profit by the ancestral powers but to admire them—much as she did the eagles overhead—and to honor them in writing. When she was 14, her maternal grandmother tried to teach her about love charms, but Mourning Dove resisted because she still wanted to remain single. Later, as a young woman, she changed her mind and sought advice from an adept elder she called Mary. "My friend," she confided, "I am poor in the knowledge of herbs, and men do not seem to care for me." Mary took her up into the hills, where the two built a sweat lodge and purified themselves before visiting a field of wildflowers, whose roots were said to have great power over human affections. Mary picked and pulverized the root and mixed it with other potent substances, including bits of "male and female green crickets for attraction." Then she taught Mourning Dove to enact the charm by speaking a man's name and praying to him: "You will think of me just as the sun rises. . . . You will come to me with love in your heart."

At the time, Mourning Dove had no man she desired, so she tried out the charm on two vain men she wanted to humble, and it seemed to have an effect. One of her targets, a Canadian mounted policeman, spent so much time visiting her on the reservation that the tribal police detained him for trespassing. Her medicine later became contaminated, and she never was able to use it on someone she cared for. But she was less intent on improving her prospects than on learning of the plant and animal powers her people cherished. She noted that even the Catholics on the reservation, who were urged by priests to spurn love charms, continued to view them as blessings from God, "bestowed upon our ancestors centuries ago."

Mourning Dove, shown at right about 1933 holding a copy of her book "Coyote Stories," grew up in the late 1800s amid the rugged hills of the Colville Reservation in eastern Washington State (above). She had to travel far as a girl to attend a Catholic mission school, but part of the land allotted to her family by the federal government in the early 1900s was donated to the community to make room for this local schoolhouse.

As a child, Mourning Dove spent several years in a Catholic school on the reservation. When her father first left her there in the care of a nun, the sight of the sister's "lovely, tapered fingers" only made her long for the touch of her mother's "careworn hands." In the end, she learned far more at home than in class. Even her knowledge of English was largely a family matter, for her parents adopted a white orphan, and Mourning Dove learned to converse with him and read the dime novels he collected. She later began writing stories about the tribal world she knew and loved. In 1927, when she was in her early forties, she was hailed as the first Indian woman novelist for a book entitled *Cogewea, The Half-Blood,* set on the Flathead Reservation in western Montana, which she had visited. Her manuscript had been so thoroughly revised by her editor, however, that she termed the published novel "someone else's book and not mine at all." Dismayed, she turned away from fiction and composed a faithful account of her life and traditions—a vivid memoir that remained in manuscript form for more than a half-century after her death in 1936 before anthropologist Jay Miller prepared it for publication.

Mourning Dove saw one other work of hers published before she died—*Coyote Stories,* a collection of tribal tales that appeared in 1933. Unlike *Cogewea,* the book was edited in a way that preserved her intent. In the lead story, she portrayed Coyote, the fabled trickster of Indian lore, as a callous husband with crude ambitions. After learning that the Spirit Chief was about to dispense new names to all the animals, Coyote informed his meek wife that he would claim the title Grizzly Bear. "Then I can devour my enemies with ease," he told her. "And I shall need you no longer. You are growing too old and homely to be the wife of a great warrior and chief." His wife went to bed without saying a word and rose early the next morning to receive an apt title from the Spirit Chief—Mole. Her husband overslept, and by the time he reached the Chief's lodge, Grizzly Bear and all the other great names had been taken, and he remained the old Coyote.

In the end, one distinctive name was left unclaimed by the animals—Quilsten, or Warmer, the title people would use thereafter to refer to their cherished sweat lodge. The wife of the Spirit Chief was kind enough to adopt that name, because she felt sorry for humans and wanted to warm their hearts. The poles of the sweat lodge represented her ribs, and all who entered felt her soothing presence. "She cannot be seen," Mourning Dove wrote, "but she always is near. Songs to her are sung by the present generation. She hears them. She hears what her people say, and in her heart there is love and pity."

Mourning Dove was just one of many writers who perpetuated the Native American tradition of wisdom keeping. Much as tribal elders sometimes adopted anthropologists and conveyed through them a cultural legacy, Indian chroniclers adopted the English language and used it to transmit their heritage. Among the versatile native writers of recent times who applied the lessons of the past were John Joseph Mathews of the Osage, author of several books retracing his own experience and that of his people; Ella Deloria of the Dakota Sioux, who explored her ancestral traditions in the novel *Waterlily* and in studies of Dakota language and lore that she conducted as an assistant to anthropologist Franz Boas; and her nephew, Vine Deloria Jr., who has argued for the right of Indians to control their own destiny politically and spiritually in such books as *Custer Died for Your Sins* and *God Is Red.*

Perhaps no modern writer found more ways to preserve and honor tribal cultures than D'Arcy McNickle, who distinguished himself as an administrator and organizer for reservation dwellers, as a scholar, and as a storyteller, whose fiction set a high standard for younger Indian novelists. Like many Native American authors in an era of increased contact between cultures, McNickle was of mixed ancestry. The son of an Irish father and a Métis mother—whose background was part Cree and part French Canadian—McNickle valued his European heritage, but he grew up largely among Indians and came to define himself as one. His mother's parents had fled Canada after the failed Métis revolt there in 1885 and settled on the Flathead Reservation. In 1905, a year after he was born, his father asked tribal leaders to admit his wife and children as members of the tribe, thus allowing them to receive land by allotment that would otherwise have been sold to white settlers.

Designation as a Flathead did not resolve the vexing question of identity for McNickle. His mother, who separated from his father when the boy was eight, discouraged him from playing with other Indians and vowed to

Buffalo by the score kick up dust on the National Bison Range, located on the Flathead Reservation in western Montana. The last free-ranging bison herd in the area was rounded up and sold in 1908. Among those observing the roundup were young D'Arcy McNickle of the Flathead and Mourning Dove, both of whom evoked the tribe's land and traditions in writing.

"raise him as a white man." Authorities deemed her a bad influence on her son, and he was sent to the Salem Indian Training School in Chemawa, Oregon. He later attended the University of Montana, studied in Europe, and lived in New York City. His ancestry was not readily apparent to others, and he might have become part of white society, as his mother hoped, had he not taken on the challenge of writing a novel set on the Flathead Reservation that brought his native heritage home to him. Ironically, his mother served as the inspiration for a commanding figure in the novel who embodies the persistence of tribal ways and impels her mixed-blood son to recognize his Indian identity as something inescapable: "It was all quite near, quite a part of him: it was his necessity, for the first time." McNickle entitled his novel *The Surrounded* to convey the feelings of constraint and solidarity within the physical and cultural bounds of the reservation.

McNickle went on to help reservation dwellers by serving in the Bureau of Indian Affairs under the farsighted John Collier, who encouraged

tribal self-determination. In his work with the bureau as in his writings on Indian customs and history, McNickle was ever alert to the risks of imposing the standards and remedies of one culture on another. "Indian societies are living organisms, having survived the gravest vicissitudes," he wrote in *They Came Here First: The Epic of the American Indian.* Radical reforms or "cures" would only destroy the natural defenses of those societies. He vividly portrayed the folly of infringing on tribal prerogatives in his short story "Hard Riding," in which a government agent insists that elders set up a court to try Indians stealing cattle from the reservation herd. The elders suspect that the thieves are only out to meet their own needs and feel that locking them up would be a greater evil than the theft itself. In the end, a chief nominates three dimwitted men to preside over the court. "It is better, we think, that fools should be judges," he explains. "If people won't listen to them, no one will mind."

D'Arcy McNickle's long and eventful career served as a bridge between the reservation era and the modern period, marked by the emergence of many gifted Indian writers who claim English as a native language but continue to honor the terms of their ancestors. Among those who have excelled as writers of fiction in recent decades are Gerald Vizenor and Louise Erdrich of the Ojibwa, and Leslie Marmon Silko of Laguna Pueblo, a poet as

D'Arcy McNickle (second from left) talks with a group of Navajo leaders in 1953 at Crownpoint, New Mexico, where he administered a community development project and continued to write about tribal culture and history.

well as a novelist. One modern writer, in particular, has drawn on the ancient resources of Indian storytelling by intermingling legend, lore, and reminiscence to offer readers both wisdom and delight. N. Scott Momaday of the Kiowa, who received the Pulitzer Prize in 1969 for his novel *House Made of Dawn,* went on to explore his personal and cultural history in two remarkable chronicles—*The Way to Rainy Mountain*, tracing the journey of the Kiowa people through myth and memory; and *The Names,* recounting the family stories that defined the author and his world.

The stories that meant most to Momaday as a child were those that revealed the origins of names and the qualities they imparted to the people and places he cherished. The name Kiowa, he learned from his relatives in Oklahoma, derived from the term *kwuda,* or "coming out," a reference to the tribal origin story in which the first Kiowas came out into world one by one through a hollow log. As they struggled from that dark passageway into the light, Momaday related, they conceived of themselves as a people: "We are, and our name is *Kwuda.*"

That coming-out was the first step in a process of emergence that carried the Kiowa from the confining forests and mountains of the north to the limitless prospects of the southern Plains. Along the way, they found a path to heaven at a spot Kiowas called Tsoai, or Rock Tree, known today as Devils Tower. Momaday knew that place in the core of his being, for an elder kinsman and storyteller gave him the name Tsoai-talee (Rock Tree Boy) in honor of a fabled Kiowa youth who turned into a bear and chased his seven sisters up the great tree that grew to become Devils Tower. The deep grooves on its cliffs were the claw marks of the bear, whose sisters eluded his grasp and entered the night sky as the stars of the Big Dipper. The name Rock Tree Boy thus gave young Momaday a role in the emergence of his people, who claimed kinship with the stars and left the mountains to seek a home on the open Plains to the south, in full view of heaven. "However tenuous their well-being," he wrote, "however much they had suffered and would suffer again, they had found a way out of the wilderness."

Looking to the sky, Kiowas found names for the passing seasons. The Leonid meteor shower in November 1833 made a profound impression on them. Pictures of shooting stars represented that year in the calendars they kept as records, and the event lived on in tribal lore as the Winter of Falling Stars. To Momaday, it marked the beginning of the "historical period" for the Kiowa, who were just then coming into contact with Anglo-Americans and would soon have to live within limits imposed on them by the federal government. The meteor shower seemed to presage the "sudden and vio-

A massive wooden sculpture completed in 1983 by Haida artist Bill Reid portrays Raven coaxing the first humans out of a shell. In Haida legend, Raven lured the people not with his harsh voice but with a soft crooning that proved irresistible.

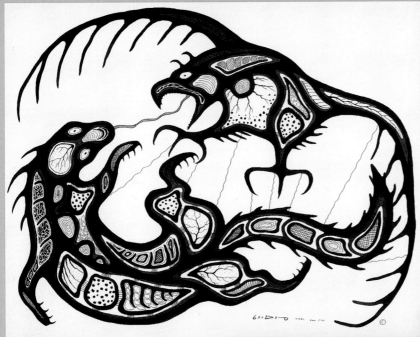

An eagle vies with a lizardlike creature in this 1975 painting by Cree artist Carl Ray entitled "Conflict between Good and Evil," evoking tribal tales of a primal struggle.

A giant emerges from stone in this work carved out of steatite by sculptor Joseph Jacobs of the Cayuga Iroquois. In Iroquois lore, stone giants were dreaded creatures who could devour humans but sometimes spared people and fostered in them skills such as carving.

REVIVING ANCIENT ACCOUNTS

Today more than ever, Indian artists are intent on celebrating the lore that forms the foundation of their tribal history. In part, these artistic efforts are an attempt to counteract the erosion of the oral tradition that long conveyed legends and sacred stories from one generation to the next. The work of Cree painter Carl Ray, for example, is part of a conscious effort by native Canadian artists in recent decades to preserve the lore of the past "before all is lost in the void of the white man's civilization," as Ray put it.

At the same time, however, artists like Ray and Bill Reid and Joseph Jacobs of the Iroquois are reinterpreting the legends. Every generation must discover their origins anew and draw fresh life from the old stories—much as Raven did in Haida legend when he spied the first humans inside a crusty shell and "coaxed and cajoled and coerced the little creatures to come out and play in his wonderful shiny new world."

lent disintegration of an old order." But even that unsettling omen was cherished in memory by Kiowas as a message from the kindred stars.

Much as Momaday relived past events through their acquired legends or titles, he communed with ancestors through the names and stories attached to them. His paternal grandfather, Mammedaty (Walking Above), from whom the family name Momaday derived, died before the author was born, but the boy came to know him well. "He enters into my dreams," Momaday wrote, "he persists in his name." Mammedaty grew up in the late 1800s, by which time Kiowa resistance to federal authorities had been crushed and the buffalo had disappeared. In this painful era of transition, he heeded the hard lessons of family elders, including the noted war chief Guipagho (Lone Wolf), who urged Kiowas to face defeat and make the best of reservation life. Mammedaty learned to "swallow his pride and be proud of it," his grandson wrote, and he took up farming even while continuing to honor the ancestral spirits as a peyote priest. He bequeathed to his descendants both a reverence for the old ways and a willingness to venture down untried paths.

The author's father, Alfred Momaday, reflected that varied inheritance. He was steeped in the oral and pictorial traditions of the Kiowa and built on them to become an accomplished artist, eventually providing the illustrations for *The Way to Rainy Mountain*. But as a young man he also longed for a life beyond the tribal circle. Like Charles Eastman, he sought success in the outside world, not as a way of renouncing his heritage but as a test of his "courage and strength," as his son put it.

In 1933 Alfred Momaday married a young woman who represented much that he admired in the larger American society, with its bracing diversity. Natachee Scott, the author's mother, was primarily of Anglo-American descent, but she owed her first name to her Cherokee great-grandmother. For Natachee as for many people in the author's family, that named prefigured her destiny. In her teens, she defined herself as an Indian and attended an Indian school, the Haskell Institute in Kansas. When Alfred Momaday later brought her home to Oklahoma to meet his Kiowa kin, however, they spurned her as an outsider. Her position there resembled that of her husband's great-grandmother, a Mexican who had been captured by Kiowas as a child. Both faced initial hostility from the family but earned respect, if not affection, by refusing to give way. "My mother stood up to the Kiowas," Momaday noted; "it was not in her to be run over."

Not long after Momaday was born, his parents left Oklahoma with their only child to live and work in the desert Southwest. But he returned

Seven stars fall from the sky in this illustration by Alfred Momaday evoking both the historic Leonid meteor shower of November 1833 and a legend of the Kiowa telling of their kinship to the seven stars of the Big Dipper. The artist depicted the scene for "The Way to Rainy Mountain," written by his son, N. Scott Momaday, who set out to explore his Kiowa heritage in terms "legendary as well as historical, personal as well as cultural."

regularly to Oklahoma to visit his grandmother Aho, her stepfather Pohd-lohk (Old Wolf)—who kept a calendar of Kiowa history beginning with the Winter of Falling Stars and gave Momaday the name Rock Tree Boy—and other elders who welcomed the youngster into their convivial round of feasting and storytelling. "There would be old men and old women in my life," he wrote gratefully. Through them, he became conversant with such ancient and storied figures as Saynday, the fabled trickster and fool of Kiowa lore, who proved so inept as a hunter that his wife ran after him with a broom and chased him up into the night sky. "There he is now in the moon," Momaday was told, "and he will not come down because he is afraid of his wife."

Those summers among the Kiowa were a great gift for him as a writer. But he was doubly blessed when his parents went to work as teachers at Jemez Pueblo in New Mexico and he entered another Indian culture rich in lore and ceremonies. In the mid-19th century, the people at Jemez had welcomed into their midst the last members of the declining Pecos Pueblo. Like those Pecos fugitives, Momaday and his parents were freely adopted by the Jemez community. When Momaday was 13 and received his first horse, he named it Pecos and cared for it with all the concern of one who knew what it was like to be adrift in a strange world and kindly taken in. In Jemez, as in Oklahoma, he found his way through the grace of others, and he returned that favor as a writer by sharing with his audience all that he had come into.

At the conclusion of *The Names,* Momaday offers readers his world by carrying them on a quest reminiscent of Black Elk's vision—a dream ride back across the Plains to Oklahoma and thence to the author's ancestral land in the north, where his horse bears him up above the circling eagles to the "top of the world" and he can see below the hollow log from which his people emerged. That haunting homeward journey fulfills a pledge voiced earlier by Momaday in the form of a prayer that came to him one day as he rode hopefully from Jemez: "Let there be wonderful things along the way; let me hold to the way and be thoughtful in my going; let this journey be made in beauty and belief." ◆

Since ancient times, dance has been a way for Indians to tell of their traditions and affirm their beliefs. Sacred observances such as the Sun Dance once brought entire tribes together to testify as one in spectacular demonstrations of fervor and finery. Among the Kiowa, all those on hand "wore splendid things—beautiful buckskin and beads," related an elder called Kosahn. "The chiefs wore necklaces, and their pendants shone like the sun."

Those great ceremonies declined during the reservation era, but Native Americans never stopped dancing. Tribal members continued to gather at powwows to dance and display their costumes. And recently, some of the finest performers found a showcase for their talents with the establishment of the American Indian Dance Theatre, founded in 1987 by Barbara Schwei, a New York theatrical producer, and Hanay Geiogamah, a Kiowa playwright and UCLA theater professor. The troupe includes some two dozen accomplished dancers, drummers, and singers from a variety of tribes, who adapt powwow favorites such as the Plains Fancy Dance *(left)* to the stage. Resplendent in their dazzling outfits, they have delighted audiences throughout the United States and abroad. Roused by the beat of the drum and the spirit of the songs, the dancers leap, twist, and weave their way through a host of intricate steps and bring the legends of their people to life.

Director Geiogamah is currently leading his dancers in a fresh direction by melding traditional steps with modern dance. To him, a willingness to adopt new ways is itself an honored tradition: "Our Indian world-view has always been flexible and accommodating to change."

Above, the Fancy Shawl or Butterfly Dance, of Plains origin, tells the story of women who, upon losing their mates in battle, retreat like caterpillars into their shawls or cocoons, only to emerge later, butterfly-like, in a new guise, happy and free. At right, dancers wear elaborately carved wooden masks for the Kwakiutl Red Cedar Bark Dance. They represent two mythical birds, Raven and Crooked Beak of Heaven, who pursue a young initiate in this rite of passage.

In the dramatic Eagle Dance, a group of performers solemnly imitate the winged flight of this most sacred and powerful of birds. The dance originated among Plains Indians to express their reverence for the eagle as a messenger linking them with the Creator above.

In the Apache Crown Dance, Mountain Spirit (far left) acts out a healing ceremony with his wands while the clown beside him prances around, mimicking him. In the Shield Dance (right), two armed warriors, richly adorned with eagle feathers, engage in mock combat in a ceremony of Plains origin celebrating the supreme challenge of hand-to-hand competition.

ACKNOWLEDGMENTS

The editors wish to thank the following individuals and institutions for their valuable assistance.

In Denmark:
  Copenhagen—Berete Due, Department of Ethnography, The National Museum of Denmark.
In France:
  Paris—Muguette Dumont, Musée de l'Homme.
In Germany:
  Berlin—Peter Bolz, Staatliche Museen zu Berlin-Preussischer Kulturbesitz, Museum für Völkerkunde. Stuttgart—Sonja Schierle, Linden-Museum.
In Russia:

St. Petersburg—Evropeisky Dom Publishers.
In the United States:
  Arizona: Phoenix—Richard Pearce-Moses, The Heard Museum.
  California: Stanford—Charles Junkerman, Stanford Humanities Center, Stanford University.
  Colorado: Denver—Cynthia Nakamura, The Denver Art Museum.
  Maryland: Gaithersburg—Antoinette McNickle Vogel.
  Massachusetts: Amherst—Barry O'Connell. Cambridge—Martha Labell, Photographic Archives, Peabody Museum of Archaeology and Ethnology, Harvard University.
  Minnesota: St. Paul—Sherri Gebert Fuller, Min-

nesota Historical Society.
  Missouri: St. Louis—Deborah Brown, Missouri Historical Society.
  Nebraska: Lincoln—John Carter, Nebraska State Historical Society. Omaha—Larry K. Mensching, Joslyn Art Museum. Tekamah—Hilda Neihardt.
  New York: New York—Barbara Schwei, American Indian Dance Theatre. Rochester—Karl Kabelac, Department of Rare Books and Special Collections, Rush Rhees Library, University of Rochester.
  Oklahoma: Anadarko—Linda Poolaw. Edmund—William Wallo, University of Central State. Tulsa—David B. Gabel, Philbrook Museum of Art.
  Washington State: Seattle—Lois Flury; Jay Miller. Spokane—Lynn Pankonin, Cheney Cowles Museum.

BIBLIOGRAPHY

BOOKS

Apess, William. *On Our Own Ground: The Complete Writings of William Apess, a Pequot.* Ed. by Barry O'Connell. Amherst: The University of Massachusetts Press, 1992.

Archuleta, Margaret, and Rennard Strickland, eds. *Shared Visions: Native American Painters and Sculptors in the Twentieth Century.* New York: The New Press, 1993.

Atlas of the Lewis & Clark Expedition. Ed. by Gary E. Moulton. Lincoln: University of Nebraska Press, 1983.

Babcock, Barbara A., Doris Monthan, and Guy Monthan. *The Pueblo Storyteller: Development of a Figurative Ceramic Tradition.* Tucson: University of Arizona Press, 1986.

Berkhofer, Robert F., Jr. *The White Man's Indian: Images of the American Indian from Columbus to the Present.* New York: Alfred A. Knopf, 1978.

Bieder, Robert E. *Science Encounters the Indian, 1820-1880: The Early Years of American Ethnology.* Norman: University of Oklahoma Press, 1986.

Black Elk. *Black Elk Speaks: Being the Life Story of a Holy Man of the Oglala Sioux.* Lincoln: University of Nebraska Press, 1988 (reprint of 1932 edition).

Boas, Franz:
  The Central Eskimo. Lincoln: University of Nebraska Press, 1964.
  The Ethnography of Franz Boas: Letters and Diaries of Franz Boas Written on the Northwest Coast from 1886 to 1931. Comp. and ed. by Ronald P. Rohner, trans. by Hedy Parker. Chicago: University of Chicago Press, 1969.

Brumble, H. David, III. *An Annotated Bibliography of American Indian and Eskimo Autobiographies.* Lincoln: University of Nebraska Press, 1981.

Cabeza de Vaca, Alvar Núñez. *Adventures in the Unknown Interior of America.* Trans. by Cyclone Covey. New York: Crowell-Collier, 1961.

Campisi, Jack. *The Mashpee Indians: Tribe on Trial.* Syracuse, N.Y.: Syracuse University Press, 1991.

Cardozo, Christopher, ed. *Native Nations: First Americans As Seen by Edward S. Curtis.* Boston: Little, Brown, 1993.

Catlin, George:
  *Episodes from Life among the Indians and Last

Rambles.* Ed. by Marvin C. Ross. Norman: University of Oklahoma Press, 1959.
  Letters and Notes on the Manners, Customs, and Conditions of the North American Indians. 2 vols. New York: Dover Publications, 1973.

Curtis, Edward S. *Portraits from North American Indian Life.* New York: Outerbridge & Lazard, 1972.

Cushing, Frank Hamilton. *Zuñi: Selected Writings of Frank Hamilton Cushing.* Ed. by Jesse Green. Lincoln: University of Nebraska Press, 1979.

Deloria, Vine, Jr. *Custer Died for Your Sins: An Indian Manifesto.* New York: Macmillan, 1969.

DesJarlait, Patrick. *Patrick DesJarlait: Conversations with a Native American Artist.* Comp. by Neva Williams. Minneapolis: Runestone Press, 1995.

Drake, Samuel G. *Indian Captivities: Or, Life in the Wigwam.* New York: AMS Press, 1975 (reprint of 1851 edition).

Dunn, Dorothy. *American Indian Painting of the Southwest and Plains Areas.* Albuquerque: University of New Mexico Press, 1968.

Eastman, Charles Alexander:
  From the Deep Woods to Civilization: Chapters in the Autobiography of an Indian. Boston: Little, Brown, 1925.
  Indian Boyhood. Williamstown, Mass.: Corner House Publishers, 1975 (reprint of 1902 edition).
  The Soul of the Indian: An Interpretation. Boston: Houghton Mifflin, 1911.

Eastman, Mary. *Dahcotah: Or, Life and Legends of the Sioux around Fort Snelling.* Minneapolis: Ross & Haines, 1962.

Events in Indian History: Beginning with an Account of the Origin of the American Indians, and Early Settlements in North America, and Embracing Concise Biographies of the Principal Chiefs and Head-Sachems of the Different Indian Tribes, with Narratives and Captivities. Lancaster, Pa.: G. Hills, 1841.

Federal Writers' Project. *California: A Guide to the Golden State.* New York: Hastings House Publishers, 1939.

Feest, Christian F. *Native Arts of North America.* New York: Thames and Hudson, 1992.

Fire, John/Lame Deer, and Richard Erdoes. *Lame Deer: Seeker of Visions.* New York: Simon and Schuster, 1972.

Fletcher, Alice C., and Francis La Flesche. *The Oma-

ha Tribe.* Vol. 1. Lincoln: University of Nebraska Press, 1992.

Foreman, Carolyn Thomas. *Indian Women Chiefs.* Washington, D.C.: Zenger, 1954.

Frederick, Joan. *T. C. Cannon: He Stood in the Sun.* Flagstaff, Ariz.: Northland Publishing, 1995.

Frost, John. *Frost's Pictorial History of Indian Wars and Captivities: From the Earliest Record of American History to the Present Time.* New York: Wells Publishing, 1873.

Gay, E. Jane. *With the Nez Perces: Alice Fletcher in the Field, 1889-92.* Ed. by Frederick E. Hoxie and Joan T. Mark. Lincoln: University of Nebraska Press, 1981.

Grumet, Robert Steven. "Sunksquaws, Shamans, and Tradeswomen: Middle Atlantic Coastal Algonkian Women during the 17th and 18th Centuries." In *Women and Colonization: Anthropological Perspectives.* Ed. by Mona Etienne and Eleanor Leacock. New York: Praeger, 1980.

Gulick, Bill. *Chief Joseph Country: Land of the Nez Perce.* Caldwell, Idaho: Caxton Printers, 1981.

Hegeman, William R., ed. *Patrick DesJarlait and the Ojibwe Tradition.* St. Paul: Minnesota Museum of American Art, 1995.

Helm, June, ed. *Pioneers of American Anthropology: The Uses of Biography.* Seattle: University of Washington Press, 1966.

Henry, Alexander. *Travels & Adventures in Canada and the Indian Territories: Between the Years 1760 and 1776.* Ed. by James Bain. St. Clair Shores, Mich.: Scholarly Press, 1972 (reprint of 1901 edition).

Herskovits, Melville J. *Franz Boas: The Science of Man in the Making.* New York: Charles Scribner's Sons, 1953.

Highwater, Jamake. *The Sweet Grass Lives On: Fifty Contemporary North American Indian Artists.* New York: Lippincott & Crowell Publishers, 1980.

Hinsley, Curtis M. *The Smithsonian and the American Indian: Making a Moral Anthropology in Victorian America.* Washington, D.C.: Smithsonian Institution Press, 1981.

Hirschmann, Fred. *Rock Art of the American Southwest.* Portland, Oreg.: Graphic Arts Center Publishing, 1994.

Hook, Jason. *American Indian Warrior Chiefs: Tecumseh, Crazy Horse, Chief Joseph, Geronimo.*

Poole, Dorset, United Kingdom: Firebird Books, 1989.

Hopkins, Sarah Winnemucca. *Life among the Piutes: Their Wrongs and Claims.* Bishop, Calif.: Chalfant Press, 1969 (reprint of 1883 edition).

Hoxie, Frederick E., and Harvey Markowitz. *Native Americans: An Annotated Bibliography.* Pasadena, Calif.: Salem Press, 1991.

Indios De America Del Norte: Otras Culturas De America. Madrid, Spain: Ministerio De Cultura, 1991.

Jennings, Francis. *Empire of Fortune: Crowns, Colonies, and Tribes in the Seven Years War in America.* New York: W. W. Norton, 1988.

Jonaitis, Aldona. *From the Land of the Totem Poles.* New York: American Museum of Natural History, 1988.

Jonaitis, Aldona, ed. *Chiefly Feasts: The Enduring Kwakiutl Potlatch.* New York: American Museum of Natural History, 1991.

Josephy, Alvin M., Jr. *The Patriot Chiefs: A Chronicle of American Indian Resistance.* New York: Penguin Books, 1993.

Judd, Neil M. *The Bureau of American Ethnology: A Partial History.* Norman: University of Oklahoma Press, 1967.

Lafitau, Joseph François. *Customs of the American Indians Compared with the Customs of Primitive Times.* 2 vols. Ed. and trans. by William N. Fenton and Elizabeth L. Moore. Toronto: The Champlain Society, 1974.

Lewis, Meriwether, and William Clark. *The History of the Lewis and Clark Expedition.* Vol. 1. New York: Dover Publications, 1979 (reprint of 1893 edition).

Liberty, Margot, ed. *American Indian Intellectuals.* St. Paul: West Publishing, 1978.

Lyman, Christopher M. *The Vanishing Race and Other Illusions: A New Look at the Work of Edward Curtis.* Washington, D.C.: Smithsonian Institution Press, 1982.

McDermott, John Francis. *Seth Eastman: Pictorial Historian of the Indian.* Norman: University of Oklahoma Press, 1961.

McNickle, D'Arcy:
The Hawk Is Hungry & Other Stories. Ed. by Birgit Hans. Tucson: University of Arizona Press, 1992.
The Indian Tribes of the United States: Ethnic and Cultural Survival. New York: Oxford University Press, 1962.
Runner in the Sun: A Story of Indian Maize. Albuquerque: University of New Mexico Press, 1982.
The Surrounded. Albuquerque: University of New Mexico Press, 1964.
They Came Here First: The Epic of the American Indian. Philadelphia: J. B. Lippincott, 1949.

Mark, Joan T.:
4 Anthropologists: An American Science in Its Early Years. New York: Science History Publications, 1980.
A Stranger in Her Native Land: Alice Fletcher and the American Indians. Lincoln: University of Nebraska Press, 1988.

Maurer, Evan M. *Visions of the People: A Pictorial History of Plains Indian Life.* Minneapolis: Minneapolis Institute of Arts, 1992.

Momaday, N. Scott:
The Names. New York: Harper & Row, 1976.

The Way to Rainy Mountain. Albuquerque: University of New Mexico Press, 1969.

Morgan, Lewis Henry. *League of the Iroquois.* New York: Corinth Books, 1962.

Moses, L. G., and Raymond Wilson, eds. *Indian Lives: Essays on Nineteenth- and Twentieth-Century Native American Leaders.* Albuquerque: University of New Mexico Press, 1985.

Moulton, Gary E., ed. *The Journals of the Lewis & Clark Expedition: August 25, 1804-April 6, 1805.* Lincoln: University of Nebraska Press, 1987.

Mourning Dove/Humishuma:
Cogewea, the Half-Blood. Lincoln: University of Nebraska Press, 1981 (reprint of 1927 edition).
Coyote Stories. Ed. by Heister Dean Guie. Caldwell, Idaho: Caxton Printers, 1933.

Mourning Dove: A Salishan Autobiography. Ed. by Jay Miller. Lincoln: University of Nebraska Press, 1990.

Murra, John V., ed. *American Anthropology: The Early Years.* St. Paul: West Publishing, 1976.

Namias, June. *White Captives: Gender and Ethnicity on the American Frontier.* Chapel Hill: University of North Carolina Press, 1993.

Native American Dance: Ceremonies and Social Traditions. Ed. by Charlotte Heth. Washington, D.C.: Smithsonian Institution, 1992.

Neihardt, John G. *The Sixth Grandfather.* Ed. by Raymond J. DeMallie. Lincoln: University of Nebraska Press, 1984.

Parker, Dorothy R. *A Biography of D'Arcy McNickle.* Lincoln: University of Nebraska Press, 1992.

Reid, Bill, and Robert Bringhurst. *The Raven Steals the Light.* Seattle: University of Washington Press, 1984.

Resek, Carl. *Lewis Henry Morgan, American Scholar.* Chicago: University of Chicago Press, 1960.

Rowlandson, Mary White. *A Narrative of the Captivity & Removes of Mrs. Mary Rowlandson.* Farfield, Wash.: Ye Galleon Press, 1974 (reprint of 1682 edition).

Ruoff, A. LaVonne Brown. *Literatures of the American Indian.* New York: Chelsea House Publishers, 1991.

Schulze-Thulin, Axel, comp. *Indianer der Prärien und Plains.* Stuttgart: Linden-Museum, 1987.

Scordato, Ellen. *Sarah Winnemucca: Northern Paiute Writer and Diplomat.* New York: Chelsea House Publishers, 1992.

Seaver, James Everett. *A Narrative of the Life of Mrs. Mary Jemison.* Norman: University of Oklahoma Press, 1992.

Shadbolt, Doris. *Bill Reid.* Seattle: University of Washington Press, 1986.

Smith, John. *Travels and Works of Captain John Smith: President of Virginia, and Admiral of New England, 1580-1631.* Part 2. Ed. by Edward Arber. Edinburgh: John Grant, 1910 (reprint of 1612 edition).

Standing Bear, Luther. *Land of the Spotted Eagle.* Boston: Houghton Mifflin, 1933.

Stocking, George W., Jr., ed. *Observers Observed: Essays on Ethnographic Fieldwork.* Vol. 1 of *History of Anthropology.* Madison: University of Wisconsin Press, 1983.

Tanner, Clara Lee. *Southwest Indian Painting: A Changing Art.* Tucson: University of Arizona Press, 1973.

Tanner, John. *A Narrative of the Captivity and Adventures of John Tanner: During Thirty Years Residence among the Indians in the Interior of North America.* Ed. by Edwin James. Minneapolis: Ross & Haines, 1956 (reprint of 1830 edition).

Thwaites, Reuben Gold, ed. *Early Western Travels, 1748-1846.* Vols. 23 and 24. Cleveland: Arthur H. Clark, 1906.

Tillett, Leslie, ed. *Wind on the Buffalo Grass: Native American Artist-Historians.* New York: Da Capo Press, 1976.

Tooker, Elisabeth. *Lewis H. Morgan on Iroquois Material Culture.* Tucson: University of Arizona Press, 1994.

Wade, Edwin, L., ed. *The Arts of the North American Indian: Native Traditions in Evolution.* New York: Hudson Hills Press, 1986.

White, Richard. *"It's Your Misfortune and None of My Own": A History of the American West.* Norman: University of Oklahoma Press, 1991.

Wilson, Raymond. *Ohiyesa: Charles Eastman, Santee Sioux.* Urbana: University of Illinois Press, 1983.

Woodard, Charles L. *Conversations with N. Scott Momaday.* Lincoln: University of Nebraska Press, 1989.

The World of the American Indian. Washington, D.C.: National Geographic Society, 1989.

PERIODICALS

Bates, Craig D. "The California Collection of I. G. Voznesenski." *American Indian Art,* Summer 1983.

Boas, Franz. "A Journey in Cumberland Sound and on the West Shore of Davis Strait in 1883 and 1884." *Journal of the American Geographical Society of New York,* vol. 16, 1884.

"Contemporary Algonkian Legend Painting." *American Indian Art,* Summer 1978.

Feder, Norman. "Museum Exhibition: The Jasper Grant Collection." *American Indian Art,* Summer 1985.

"Horace Poolaw: Half a Century of Kiowa Life." *Camera & Darkroom,* October 1992.

Hudson, Travis. "Early Russian-Collected California Ethnographic Objects in European Museums." *American Indian Art,* Autumn 1984.

Jones, Don H. "Harry Fonseca, Artist: Painter of Coyote Legend." *The Santa Fean,* August 1984.

Nelson, Mary Carroll. "Pablita Velarde." *American Indian Art,* Spring 1978.

Schulze-Thulin, Axel. "Linden-Museum Stuttgart." *American Indian Art,* Summer 1979.

Varjola, Pirjo, and Joyce Herold. "Early Ethnographic Collections from Alaska: An Exhibition from the National Museum of Finland." *American Indian Art,* Summer 1992.

OTHER SOURCES

Hyer, Sally. " 'Woman's Work': The Art of Pablita Velarde." Catalog. Santa Fe, N.Mex.: Wheelwright Museum of the American Indian, 1993.

"Indian Humor." Catalog. San Francisco: American Indian Contemporary Arts, 1995.

"War Bonnets, Tin Lizzies, and Patent Leather Pumps: Kiowa Culture in Transition, 1925-1955." Catalog. Stanford, Calif.: Stanford University, 1990.

PICTURE CREDIT

Credits for the illustrations from left to right are separated by semicolons, from top to bottom by dashes.

Cover: Nebraska State Historical Society. **6, 7:** Library of Congress, neg. no. USZ-62-83960; Flury and Company. **8:** Library of Congress. **9:** Library of Congress, neg. no. USZ-62-73627. **10:** Washington State Historical Society, Tacoma. **11:** Library of Congress, neg. nos. USZ-62-9532—USZ-62-52951. **12:** Library of Congress, neg. no. USZ-62-110506—Library of Congress. **13:** Library of Congress, neg. no. USZ-62-83966. **14:** Flury and Company. **15:** Washington State Historical Society, Tacoma; Library of Congress, neg. no. USZ-62-66856. **16:** Library of Congress, neg. no. USZ-62-74131—Library of Congress. **17:** Library of Congress. **18:** National Gallery of Canada, Ottawa, transfer from the Canadian War Memorials, 1921 (gift of the 2nd Duke of Westminster, Eaton Hall, Cheshire, 1918). **20:** From *Events in Indian History,* G. Hills & Co., 1841. **21, 22:** Bibliothèque Nationale de France. **23:** Courtesy Pocumtuck Valley Memorial Association, Memorial Hall Museum and Indian House Memorial, Deerfield, Mass. **24, 25:** The National Museum of Denmark, Department of Ethnography, photo by Kit Weiss. **26:** Coll. Musée de l'Homme, photo by D. Ponsard. **27:** From *Frost's Pictorial History of Indian Wars and Captivities,* by John Frost, Wells Publishing Co., 1873; courtesy Pocumtuck Valley Memorial Association, Memorial Hall Museum and Indian House Memorial, Deerfield, Mass. **29:** Map by Maryland CartoGraphics, Inc. **30:** Collection of Valerie Wooldridge. **32:** Courtesy American Antiquarian Society. **34, 35:** Courtesy of the Fruitlands Museums, Harvard, Mass.—Trustees of the Boston Public Library. **36:** Gregory K. Scott. **37:** Archive Photos, N.Y. **38, 39:** National Museums & Galleries on Merseyside, Liverpool; Oberösterreichisches Landesmuseum, Linz, Austria: Graphische Sammlung, Ha290. **41:** Linden-Museum Stuttgart, photo by Anatol Dreyer. **42, 43:** Courtesy Royal Ontario Museum, Toronto. **45:** National Anthropological Archives (NAA), Smithsonian Institution, no. 765-C. **46, 47:** From *A Narrative of the Captivity and Adventures of John Tanner,* ed. by Edwin James, G.& C.& H. Carvill, 1830. **49:** State Historical Society of Wisconsin, no. WHi(X3) 15462. **50:** Courtesy West Point Museum, USMA. **52:** Brian Scriven, Genesee State Park Region, New York State Office of Parks, Recreation and Historic Preservation. **53:** From *A Narrative of the Life of Mary Jemison: The White Woman of the Genesee,* by James Everett Seaver, The American Scenic & Historic Preservation Society, N.Y., 1925. **54:** Brian Scriven, Genesee State Park Region, New York State Office of Parks, Recreation and Historic Preservation. **55:** Courtesy of the New York State Museum, Albany, no. 36961. **56, 57:** Museo Naval, Madrid; Museo de América, Madrid. **58, 59:** Museo de América, Madrid. **60, 61:** Coll. Musée de l'Homme, photo by B. Hatala (2)—Coll. Musée de l'Homme, photo by M. Delaplanche; Coll. Musée de l'Homme, photo by D. Destable; Coll. Musée de l'Homme, photo by M. Delaplanche. **62, 63:** National Museum of Ireland, Dublin. **64, 65:** Linden-Museum Stuttgart, photo by Tamara Hannemann—Linden-Museum Stuttgart, photo by

Anatol Dreyer (2)—Linden-Museum Stuttgart, photo by Ursula Didoni. **66:** Kunstkamera, St. Petersburg. **67:** Staatliche Museum für Völkerkunde, Munich, photo by S. Autrum-Mulzer—Museum für Völkerkunde der Stadt, Frankfurt am Main, photo by Stephan Beckers. **68, 69:** National Museum of Finland, Helsinki. **70:** Joslyn Art Museum, Omaha, gift of the Enron Art Foundation. **72:** © Trustees of the British Museum, London—courtesy Independence National Historical Park, Philadelphia (2). **74:** Rare Books Division, New York Public Library. **76, 77:** Peabody Museum, Harvard University, photograph by Hillel Burger. **78:** Beinecke Rare Book & Manuscript Library, Yale University; Missouri Historical Society, St. Louis. **79:** American Philosophical Society, Philadelphia. **81:** George Catlin, *Catlin Feasted by the Mandan Chief,* Paul Mellon Collection, © 1995 Board of Trustees, National Gallery of Art, Washington, D.C. 1861/1869. **82, 84:** National Museum of American Art, Washington, D.C./Art Resource. **85:** University of Pennsylvania Museum, Philadelphia, neg. no. T4-629c.2. **86:** Joslyn Art Museum, Omaha, gift of the Enron Art Foundation. **87:** Minnesota Historical Society, St. Paul—Joslyn Art Museum, Omaha, gift of the Enron Art Foundation. **88, 89:** Joslyn Art Museum, Omaha, gift of the Enron Art Foundation. **91:** The Western Reserve Historical Society, Cleveland. **92:** Lewis Henry Morgan Papers, Department of Rare Books and Special Collections, University of Rochester Library, Rochester, N.Y. **93:** Ewell Sale Stewart Library, The Academy of Natural Sciences of Philadelphia. **94:** From *League of the Ho-de-no-sau-nee, or Iroquois,* by Lewis H. Morgan, Dodd, Mead and Co., 1904. **95:** Ewell Sale Stewart Library, The Academy of Natural Sciences of Philadelphia. **97:** Nebraska State Historical Society. **98:** Peabody Museum, Harvard University, photograph by Hillel Burger. **99:** Idaho State Historical Society, no. 3771. **100:** Peabody Museum, Harvard University, photograph by Hillel Burger. **101:** Idaho State Historical Society, neg. no. 63-221.66. **102:** From *Eighth Annual Report of the Bureau of Ethnology to the Secretary of the Smithsonian Institution,* 1886-87, by J. W. Powell, Government Printing Office, Washington, D.C., 1891. **103:** From *Second Annual Report of the Bureau of Ethnology to the Secretary of the Smithsonian Institution,* 1880-1881, by J. W. Powell, Government Printing Office, Washington, D.C., 1883—NAA, Smithsonian Institution, no. 64-A-13-A. **104:** From *Twenty-First Annual Report of the Bureau of American Ethnology to the Secretary of the Smithsonian Institution,* 1899-1900, by J. W. Powell, Government Printing Office, Washington, D.C., 1903. **106:** NAA, Smithsonian Institution, no. 22E. **107:** The Denver Public Library, Western History Department. **108:** NAA, Smithsonian Institution, no. 86-4099. **109:** From *Second Annual Report of the Bureau of Ethnology to the Secretary of the Smithsonian Institution,* 1880-1881, by J. W. Powell, Government Printing Office, Washington, D.C., 1883. **110:** Neg. no. 2A-5161, courtesy Department Library Services, American Museum of Natural History—neg. no. 11854, courtesy Department Library Services, American Museum of Natural History. **111:** Neg. no. 335772 (photo by H. Smith), courtesy Department Library Services, American Museum of Natural History. **112, 113:** Neg. no. 351, courtesy Department Library Services, American Museum of

Natural History; neg. no. 3843(2) (photo by Stephen S. Myers), courtesy Department Library Services, American Museum of Natural History. **115:** Courtesy Linda Poolaw. **116:** Photos courtesy Stanford University. **117:** Courtesy Linda Poolaw. **118-123:** Photos courtesy Stanford University. **124:** The Philbrook Museum of Art, Tulsa. **125:** Denver Art Museum. **126:** Collection of James T. Bailac, courtesy The Heard Museum, Phoenix—The Philbrook Museum of Art, Tulsa. **127:** The Philbrook Museum of Art, Tulsa. **128:** Minnesota Historical Society—collection of James T. Bailac, courtesy The Heard Museum, Phoenix. **129:** From the Collection of the Minnesota Museum of American Art. **130:** Collection of Nancy and Richard Bloch. **131:** Collection of Anne-Rachel Aberbach, courtesy T. C. Cannon Estate—Joe Pytka, courtesy T. C. Cannon Estate. **132:** Harry Fonseca—California State Indian Museum. **133:** Collection of Caryll and William Mingst, Moose, Wyo., courtesy The Heard Museum, Phoenix. **134, 135:** Carl Moon, *Tale of the Tribe,* New York Public Library. **136:** Courtesy the John G. Neihardt Trust and the Western Historical Manuscripts Collection, University of Missouri, Columbia. **137:** From *Black Elk Speaks,* by John G. Neihardt, 1932, courtesy the John G. Neihardt Trust. **138:** Reprinted from *Black Elk Speaks,* by John G. Neihardt, by permission of the University of Nebraska Press. © 1932, 1959, 1972, by John G. Neihardt. © 1961 by the John G. Neihardt Trust. **140:** Nebraska State Historical Society. **142:** Veronica Smith. **143:** From the Girard Foundation Collection, Museum of International Folk Art, a unit of the Museum of New Mexico, Santa Fe. **145:** State Historical Society of North Dakota, no. 791. **146, 147:** Coll. Musée de l'Homme, photo by B. Hatala—Fred Hirschmann, Wasilla, Alaska; Coll. Musée de l'Homme, photos by D. Ponsard (2). **148, 149:** Charles H. Barstow Collection, Eastern Montana College, photo by Michael Crummett—Mark Sexton, courtesy The Children's Museum, Boston; Werner Forman Archive, London. **150, 151:** From *A Son of the Forest: The Experience of William Apes, A Native of the Forest,* written by Himself, Second Edition, N.Y., 1831. **155:** Nevada Historical Society. **156:** © Joe Cantrell (2)—© John Hughel Jr. **158:** © 1995 Brian Seed and W. S. Nawrocki. **159:** From *Lame Deer, Seeker of Visions,* by John Fire/Lame Deer and Richard Erdoes, Simon and Shuster, N.Y., 1972. **161:** From *My People the Sioux,* by Luther Standing Bear, Houghton Mifflin Company, The Riverside Press, 1928—Denver Art Museum. **162, 163:** Courtesy W. Duncan MacMillan. **164:** Nebraska State Historical Society—James D. Ewing, Keene, N.H. **165:** Courtesy South Dakota State Historical Society. **168, 169:** Jay Miller. **171:** © Michael Crummett. **172:** Photo courtesy The Newberry Library. **174:** *The Raven and the First Men,* by Bill Reid, 1980, courtesy the UBC Museum of Anthropology, Vancouver, B.C. **175:** Carl Ray, *Conflict between Good and Evil,* 1975, McMichael Canadian Art Collection, Kleinburg, Ontario—Schoharie Museum of the Iroquois Indian. **177:** Drawing by Al Momaday from *The Way to Rainy Mountain,* by N. Scott Momaday, © 1969, the University of New Mexico Press. **178-181:** Theo Westenberger/Gamma Liaison. **182, 183:** Don Perdue. **184, 185:** Theo Westenberger/Gamma Liaison.

INDEX

Numerals in italics indicate an illustration of the subject mentioned.